THE MEEK CUTOFF

Tracing the Oregon Trail's Lost Wagon Train of 1845

THE MEEK CUTOFF

Tracing the Oregon Trail's Lost Wagon Train of 1845

BROOKS GEER RAGEN

UNIVERSITY OF WASHINGTON PRESS

Seattle and London

© 2013 by the University of Washington Press
Printed and bound in Canada
Design by Thomas Eykemans
Composed in Sorts Mill Goudy, typeface designed by Barry Schwartz
Display type set in Deming, designed by Mike Fortress
17 16 15 14 13   5 4 3 2 1

Maps by Allan Cartography

Photography by Richard Adams, Steve Lent, Art and Jane McEldowney,
Ellen Morris Bishop, Suzanne Ragen, and Lee Schaefer

UNIVERSITY OF WASHINGTON PRESS
PO Box 50096, Seattle, WA 98145, USA
www.washington.edu/uwpress

LIBRARY OF CONGRESS CATALOGING-IN-PUBLICATION DATA
Ragen, Brooks Geer, 1933–
The Meek Cutoff : tracing the Oregon trail's lost wagon train of 1845 /
Brooks Geer Ragen.
        pages cm
Includes bibliographical references and index.
ISBN 978-0-295-99309-6 (cloth : alk. paper)
1. Meek's Cutoff (Or.)
2. Overland journeys to the Pacific.
3. Meek, Stephen Hall, 1805–1889.
I. Title.
F880.R25 2013   979.5'03—dc23   2013008273

The paper used in this publication is acid-free and meets the minimum requirements of American National Standard for Information
Sciences—Permanence of Paper for Printed Library Materials, ANSI
z39.48–1984.∞

TO MY WIFE, SUSIE, WHO MAINTAINED A HIGHLY enthusiastic demeanor even though the Meek expeditions were out of her "comfort zone."

TO MY GREAT-GREAT-UNCLE, JOSEPH CAREY GEER JR., who was with the Lost Wagon Train of 1845.

TO MY GRANDMOTHER, ANNETTA "NETTIE" GEER Sweitzer Gradon, and my mother, Florence Gradon Ragen, who initiated and encouraged my interest in the story of the Meek Cutoff.

TO THOSE WHO ARE INTERESTED IN EXPLORING the historic trails and vanishing Old West of eastern Oregon.

"Go back we could not, and we knew not what was before us."

—Elizabeth (Betsy) Bayley, *The Munson Record*

*"I will just say pen and tong will both fall short when
they gow to tell the suffering the Company went through."*

—From the diary of Samuel Parker

CONTENTS

List of Maps   *viii*

Preface   *ix*

Introduction   *3*

    The Lost Wagon Train of 1845   *7*

    The Diaries, Diarists, and Reminiscences   *14*

    The Meek Research Expedition   *15*

    Meek Research Expedition Members   *21*

    The Gold   *23*

The Journey, Day to Day   *29*

Some Final Thoughts   *151*

Note on Sources   *152*

Index   *154*

MAPS

MAP 1 Oregon Trail, Missouri to Oregon 4

MAP 2 Oregon Trail, from Fort Boise
       to Oregon City 9

MAP 3 Meek Trail Overview 10

MAP 4 Route of the two Meek parties
       from Cline Falls and the Crooked River
       to The Dalles and to Oregon City 13

MAP 5 A portion of 1845 "Map of the Western
       and Middle Portion of North America" 18

MAP 6 The Hampton Buttes—
       Maury Mountains 26

MAP 7 Headwaters of the Malheur River 27

MAP 8 August 23, 1845 31

MAP 9 August 24, 1845 35

MAP 10 August 25, 1845 38

MAP 11 August 26, 1845 42

MAP 12 August 27, 1845 46

MAP 13 August 28, 1845 52

MAP 14 August 29, 1845 56

MAP 15 August 30, 1845 60

MAP 16 August 31, 1845 63

MAP 17 September 1, 1845 65

MAP 18 September 2, 1845 69

MAP 19 September 3, 1845 72

MAP 20 September 4, 1845 77

MAP 21 September 5, 1845 81

MAP 22 September 5, 1845 82

MAP 23 September 6, 1845 85

MAP 24 September 6, 1845 86

MAP 25 September 7, 1845 89

MAP 26 September 8, 1845 92

MAP 27 September 9, 1845 96

MAP 28 September 10, 1845 100

MAP 29 September 11, 1845 102

MAP 30 September 12, 1845 104

MAP 31 September 13, 1845 108

MAP 32 September 14, 1845 110

MAP 33 September 15, 1845 113

MAP 34 September 16, 1845 116

MAP 35 September 17, 1845 120

MAP 36 September 18, 1845 124

MAP 37 September 18, 1845 125

MAP 38 September 19, 1845 129

MAP 39 September 20, 1845 133

MAP 40 September 21, 1845 139

MAP 41 September 22, 1845 142

MAP 42 September 23, 1845 144

MAP 43 September 24, 1845 146

MAP 44 September 25, 1845 148

PREFACE

WHILE NATIVE AMERICANS WERE THE ORIGINAL inhabitants of that part of the American continent now known as the Pacific Northwest, Russian, Spanish, and British ships explored the area's coast on many occasions during the eighteenth century. In 1804–6, Lewis and Clark crossed the North American continent and spent the winter of 1805–6 near the present-day city of Astoria, Oregon. Commercial interests, principally the Hudson's Bay Company, a few British and American trappers, and missionaries followed; both Great Britain and America laid claim to the area; and in 1818 Great Britain and the United States signed a treaty of joint occupancy. In succeeding years, American politicians and individuals encouraged the exploration and settlement of that part of the Pacific Northwest called the Oregon country. Great Britain claimed title to the land north of the Columbia River, but appealing reports of climate and farming relayed to the East from some of those who had visited the Pacific Northwest prepared the way for increasing American interest in the entire region. In the eastern part of the United States, political and populist pressures to annex the entire territory began to build.

The slogan "54–40 or Fight," referring to the longitude politicians and the press claimed as the United States' northern boundary, popularized a major issue in the presidential election of 1844. In 1848, Great Britain and the United States signed a treaty declaring that the 49th parallel would divide the Pacific Northwest, with the British taking title to the land north of the parallel and the United States to the land on the south. The United States portion was formally designated the Oregon Territory in 1849.

Since travel by sea to the Pacific Northwest from the East was lengthy, expensive, and dangerous, the preferred route became a land trail across the continent. Those who traveled to the Pacific Northwest by land became known as overlander emigrants. The first emigrants to travel to Oregon were missionaries who left Missouri in 1836. They abandoned their wagons en route and arrived on horseback. Small groups of emigrants continued to travel west from 1837 to 1842, but the 875 people who migrated in 1843 were the first large group to travel the entire route from Independence and St. Joseph, Missouri, to the Willamette Valley in wagons. When they arrived, the settlers found only a few scattered settlements. The country was largely unoccupied. Most roads were simply trails, and the pleasantries of life in the American East were nonexistent.

About 1,475 emigrants traveled the trail in 1844 and some 2,500 traveled the route the following year. Stephen Meek, a well-known mountain man, persuaded about 1,200 of those 2,500 emigrants to leave the established route at what is now Vale, Oregon and take a shortcut across the desert of eastern Oregon to The Dalles on the Columbia River. From there, most planned to raft down the Columbia to its confluence with the Willamette River and then travel south along the river to the Willamette Valley. Meek convinced the emigrants that the shortcut would save time and would avoid inhospitable Indians and difficult topography.

Those who followed Meek experienced a terrible ordeal in their journey across eastern Oregon. While the history of that experience has been well documented by historians such as Keith Clark, Lowell Tiller, and Donna Wojcik, no one, to date, has accurately located the Meek Trail from Vale, Oregon, to the Deschutes River. This book is the result of my desire to retrace, as accurately as possible, the Meek Cutoff.

When I was a small child, my maternal grandmother and my mother often told me the story of the Meek shortcut. I remember being impressed with their description of the miserable conditions experienced by the lost emigrants and their desperate search for water and food. I was also intrigued with that part of the tale associated with a legendary gold discovery, the Blue Bucket lode, never rediscovered.

My mother's side of the family had a lengthy association with Oregon. Joseph Carey Geer, my mother's great-grandfather, emigrated in 1847 and settled in the Waldo Hills east of Salem, Oregon. His homestead, the Riding Whip Ranch, is still occupied by Geer family members. Joseph Carey Geer Jr. (1825–1909), a son of my great-great-grandfather Joseph Carey Geer, was an emigrant with the Meek Cutoff wagon train.

For years, I have collected books, diaries, and other materials that refer to the Lost Wagon Train, a name popularized by numerous reminiscences, newspaper articles, letters to the editor, and several books. In the spring of 2006, I decided to sponsor an expedition to trace Meek's Cutoff, to walk the actual trail and link the scenes and events described in the diaries and reminiscences with the landscape. To help me in this endeavor, I was fortunate enough to bring together specialists in a variety of fields, including geology, global positioning, metal detecting, history, and photography. We wanted, if possible, to locate wagon ruts, grave sites, drag logs (a log, brush, or other impediment attached to the rear of a wagon to slow its descent down a steep slope), and more. We wanted to focus on the most difficult and least-known part of the trail—from Vale, Oregon, to the upper reaches of the Crooked River and/or to a location near Bend or Redmond, Oregon, where a section of the train reportedly reached the Deschutes River. In fact, the train split at the springs on the present-day GI Ranch, one part traveling north to the Crooked River and down that river. The other section traveled west along the south slope of the Maury Mountains and then to the Deschutes River at Cline Falls near Redmond, Oregon. Those groups united at Sagebrush Springs, south of present-day Madras. It was during this period of their journey that the travelers were lost and desperate for food and water. When they reached the Crooked and Deschutes Rivers, they had some idea of their location and they had water for people and animals. Even though records indicate more deaths occurred after the parties reached the Crooked and Deschutes, I suspect most of those deaths resulted from the extreme suffering experienced during the period the emigrants were lost in the high desert of eastern Oregon.

ACKNOWLEDGMENTS

There are some people, and I am one, who feel an inexpressible need to walk where the emigrants walked, imagine their difficulties and successes, and try to recapture the landscape of an undeveloped American West. The diaries, maps, photographs, and notes from feet on the ground published here are all an effort to help make these people and their experiences live again. Our team attempted to be where the diarists were the day they wrote their diary entries over 160 years ago.

To recreate the story we had to determine, as accurately as possible, the geography of the land the emigrants of the Meek wagon train traveled and to reflect on their observations about the land, the Native Americans they met, and their concerns about their leader and fellow travelers. It was a daunting challenge.

When I started this project, I realized I would need the assistance of many people, including historians, scholars, experts in specific fields, and ranchers. If anything, I underestimated the help needed.

There are no words to express my appreciation for the contribution of expedition members. In a most serendipitous fashion, I met, became friends with, and engaged some extraordinary people. A personal friendship with two team members led to meetings with several other individuals who expressed a real enthusiasm for my project. Specialists in metal detecting (Margi Heater and Paul Cronin), geopositioning (Art and Jane McEldowney), eastern Oregon history and geography (Bob Boyd and Steve Lent), and, of course, photography (Ellen Morris Bishop and Lee Schaefer) were essential. Photographs of the team members and short biographical sketches can be found later in the text. Their unswerving loyalty to the project over several years was remarkable and I am indebted to each of them.

I've borrowed liberally and shamelessly from Keith Clark and Lowell Tiller's *Terrible Trail: The Meek Cutoff, 1845* and Donna Wojcik's *The Brazen Overlanders of 1845*. Without these books as guides, this job would have been overwhelming for a businessman with many obligations. Delmar Hinshaw's maps and comments were essential. Of course, the diarists themselves and their annotators were invaluable. Permission to use the heretofore unpublished Cooley diary was most important, particularly when we were following that part of the train that traveled south of the Maury Mountains and eventually reached the Deschutes River at Cline Falls near Redmond.

Howard Lamar, Yale University's retired interim president and one of the most respected historians of the American West, strongly encouraged me to persevere and complete the project when numerous discouraging delays and problems surfaced in preparation and mapping.

Jim Meacham, head of the University of Oregon's Cartography Department, gave valuable help envisioning the project, and his introduction to Stuart Allan was essential to this work. Stuart, an internationally acclaimed cartographer in Medford, Oregon, prepared the maps with the help of his staff at Allan Cartography. Without question, the maps are a highlight of this book. It was my good fortune to become acquainted with Norman Wright, professor emeritus at Brigham Young University and an authority on odometers. Recorded distances in the diaries, an important part of the story, often seemed in error. Dr. Wright's explanation of the workings of pioneer odometers helped explain the difficulty of accurate distance measurement in the nineteenth century. Several researchers at the Oregon California Trails Association, the Oregon Historical Society, and the Seattle Public Library gave needed assistance. Specifically, I would like to thank Blynne Olivieri, Pacific Northwest Curator, University of Washington Libraries, and Kay Kovacks, Glenda J. Pearson, and Jim Stack of the Suzzallo Library at the University of Washington; Kreg Hawegawa and Jeannette Voiland of the Seattle Public Library; and Sandra Crittenden and Karen Nitz of the Harney County Library for their generous assistance on specific issues.

Descendants of the Cooley family, including Margi Heater and Grace Remington, were most helpful in getting permission to print the previously unpublished Cooley diary. John Zancanella of the Prineville Bureau of Land Management office reviewed and corrected my comments on the requirements for on-the-ground research in the high desert of eastern Oregon. Bill Smith, a longtime friend and successful Bend entrepreneur, generously lent me his personal off-road vehicle and encouraged me to stay at his Bend-area condominium before and after each expedition.

My thanks to Ellen Waterston and to my son, Cam, and grandson, Jackson, who spent several days accompanying the expedition.

The following ranches, ranch owners, and managers, who allowed the expedition to cross their properties, made the whole effort possible. These include, running from east to west: the Butler Beulah Ranch (Bill, Anita, and Robin Butler); the Castle Rock Ranch (Joe Villagrana); the Turner Ranch (Tom Turner); O'Toole Ranch (Pat O'Toole); the Cow Creek Ranch (Dan Toelle); Mortimer Canyon (Jack Smith); the Double O Ranch (Georgia and Gary Marshall); the Wagontire Ranch (John Piela); the GI Ranch (Bill Smith and the Kennedy family); the Les Schwab Ranch; the McCormack Ranch (Bill McCormack); the Rubbert ranch (formerly known as the Coffelt Ranch or Nye Ranch—maps generally show the name Cofelt, while local usage is "Coffelt"—Wendy Rubbert, owner; Jim and Lorraine

Walters, managers); the Salt Creek Ranch (Jim Kordahl, owner; Jean Nelson, resident caretaker; Cy Flack, cowboy, and Sarah Larson, local history buff, provided access to Alkali Butte); and last, the Dunham Ranch (now known as the Bear Creek Ranch, owned by Ron Miller, Kurt Lockhart, manager).

Others who assisted along the way include Togo and Beverly Dice, who tried to prepare us for the difficulties in getting to Swamp Creek. I am also indebted to Bob and Brad Jordan, associated with the Bully Creek Reservoir Park, who were very knowledgeable about that part of the train that traveled up Bully Creek. Kim Hanson of Seattle helped me select and integrate photographs with the day-to-day story.

Acquiring editor Marianne Keddington-Lang sponsored my manuscript at the University of Washington Press. Her comments and suggestions greatly improved the readability of this book. I am deeply indebted to her; to Julidta Tarver, former managing editor at UW Press, who served as copyeditor; to designer Thomas Eykemans; and to managing editor Marilyn Trueblood, who provided overall leadership for the project.

Esther Holt, my personal assistant, used her substantial skills, and exhibited extraordinary patience over the several years of this project. Esther, originally from eastern Oregon, had an interest in the story and her suggested changes and improvements are reflected throughout the book. Without her continuous help and advice, I could not have completed this project.

THE MEEK CUTOFF

Tracing the Oregon Trail's Lost Wagon Train of 1845

INTRODUCTION

FROM 1840 TO 1860, AN ESTIMATED FIFTY THOU-sand people traveled overland across the American continent to what became designated as the Oregon Territory. The journey from the Missouri River departure points to Oregon's Willamette Valley averaged about 166 days—five and a half months—on the trail, during 1841 to 1849. Travel on the Oregon Trail increased during the 1850s and 1860s, but with the completion of the first transcontinental railroad in 1869 activity on the trail declined. Travelers could take the train to California and then journey by steamer up the Pacific coast to Oregon. In 1883, the Northern Pacific Railroad reached Portland, Oregon, and travelers could make the entire journey by rail.

The vast majority of emigrants moved in response to an extremely successful public relations campaign conducted by politicians, the press, missionaries, and emigrant societies. "Paradise was worth a long and dangerous trip and it was paradise which the promoters were selling," historian John Unruh concludes in *The Plains Across*. Who were the travelers of the Oregon Trail? Unruh suggests that many were people inured to strenuous physical exertion, such as farmers, who were more capable of accepting the hardships of overland travel than were prospective settlers from urban locations. Unruh tends to downplay the familiar stereotypical qualifiers of hardships and dangers associated with overland travel. He believes that the hardship theory was spawned and promoted by

the press of the 1840s and 1850s and flowered under the aegis of the pioneer associations formed in the 1870s and 1880s when every survivor made his account of the trip seem more arduous than others. Unruh stresses the cooperative relationship between the emigrants and the Indians and among the emigrants themselves. There were many whose reports and diaries stressed the adventure, heroism, and excitement of the trip. On the other hand, Unruh cites the stories of the Donner and Meek groups as examples of major tragedies on the trail. The infamous Donner Party included emigrants headed overland to California who were delayed due to a series of mishaps. They spent the winter of 1846–47 snowbound in the Sierra Nevada, some apparently resorting to cannibalism to survive. With those parties, the hardship was real and the suffering the basis of legend. In concluding his book, Unruh commends even those overlanders who allegedly had it easy: "The energy, perseverance, and courage of the overland emigrants are as impressive today as they were in the 1840s and 1850s. It is no wonder that those who completed the adventure wrote and spoke about it often in subsequent years. It was something to be proud of." They risked their lives and their modest tangible assets and were willing to cut their ties with friends and relations, often forever, to make a new home in a largely unknown land.

Westward emigration always began in the spring when grass was abundant and rivers were subsiding

from the winter runoff. Trains ranging in size from twenty to one hundred wagons usually departed from two communities in Missouri. "Hunters and trappers were coming from and going to the great western country—St. Joe and Independence, Missouri were the starting points for travelers. They called it the Oregon fever and to those living so close to the trail (Platt Co., Mo.) it was most contagious." This quote comes from a typewritten document furnished to the author by Donna Wojcik. The attribution reads "Probably from Tetherow Journal—members of Cumberland Presbyterian Church." The document accurately describes much of the interest and excitement associated with the opening of the American West.

John Unruh summarizes some of the characteristics of the travelers as well as costs of the trip and health concerns that had to be considered by the emigrants. Most emigrants were farmers or had a farming background. While a large majority of overlanders came from the American Midwest, the largest percentage came from Missouri. Trip expenses varied widely. There is some agreement, however, that the initial expenses for the trip ranged from one hundred to two hundred dollars per emigrant. In addition, cash of fifty to two hundred dollars was recommended for expenses on the trail. Such expenses might include bridge and ferry fees, trading post expenditures, and purchases of goods and food from other travelers. Diseases and accidents were major health problems. Cholera, mountain

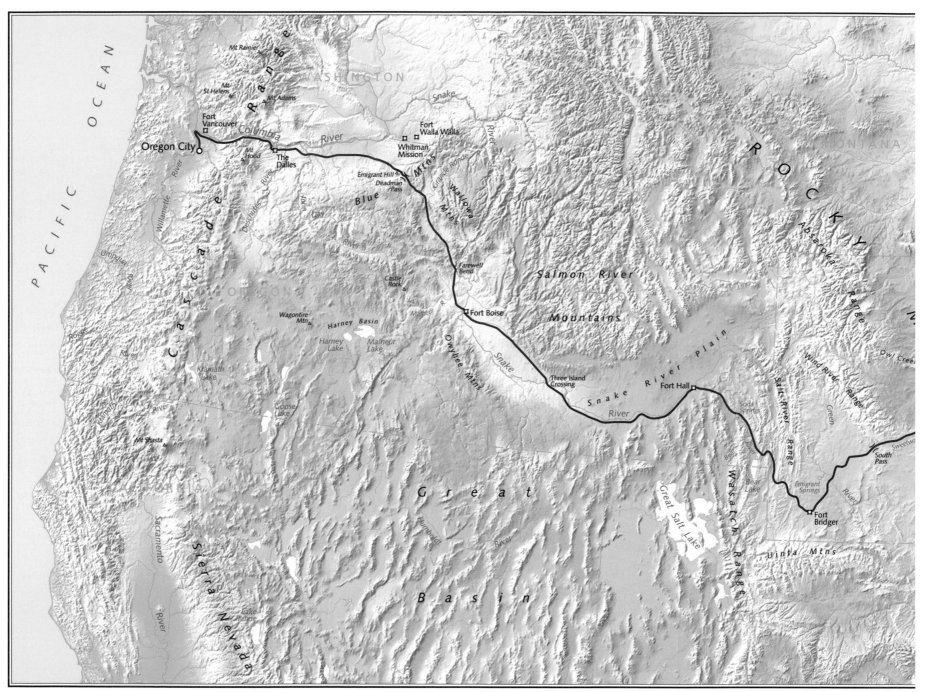

MAP 1 Oregon Trail, Missouri to Oregon

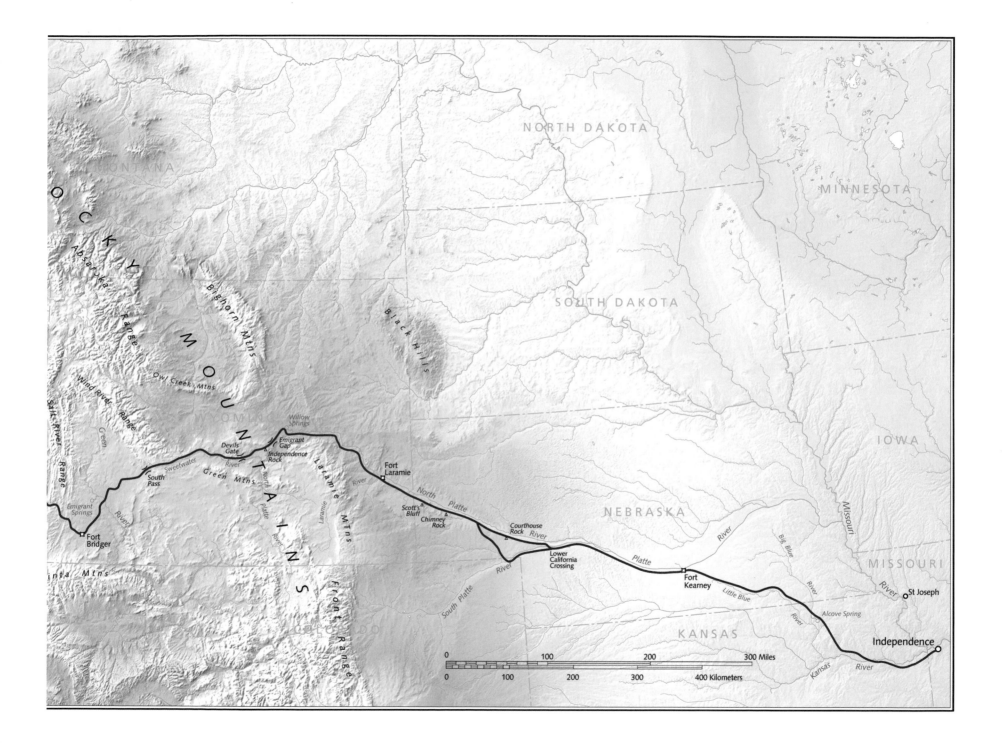

fever, smallpox, and scurvy killed many emigrants. Accidents and disease were responsible for most deaths on the trail. Indian attacks, while much feared, were generally a minor problem. Unruh believes that trail mortality from all causes was around 4 percent.

The emigrants usually joined together in small groups or companies. Pre-existing friendships and extended family relations played a role in the composition of the various companies. Numerous groups included several generations of the same family.

Before or shortly after departure, the companies often determined their governance by adopting a written constitution and electing officers. The leadership group usually included a captain, treasurer, secretary, lieutenants, and other officials with attendant responsibilities such as safety, hunting, scouting, and legal matters. Bylaws governing conduct on the trail were usually adopted. Males over the age of sixteen who subscribed to the constitution and paid a one-dollar initiation fee could become members of the company. Those who became members placed themselves under the authority of the elected officers of the company.

The first constitution of the 1845 emigration was prepared and adopted on April 5, 1845. Amendments were incorporated in a subsequent document dated May 5 and titled the Oregon Society Constitution. Articles include:

Art. 1st This society shall be known by [sic] the Oregon emigrating Company.
Art. 2nd The majority in all cases shall rule.
Art. 4th The Officers & men shall come under the Military law of the United States.
Art. 5th Any man going to sleep on duty or deserting his post without leave The executive Council shall determine the fine or punishment.

The bylaws, apparently adopted on the same day or a few days later, are particularly interesting. Some examples:

Anyone guilty of wilful murder shall be punished by death and shall not be forced into trial before three days.

Anyone guilty of manslaughter shall be delivered to the authorities in Oregon.

Any one guilty of Rape or attempt at it shall receive thirty nine lashes for three successive days—

Any one guilty of open adultery, or fornication shall receive 39 lashes on their bare back.

Any one guilty of indecent language shall be fined at the discretion of the Ex. Counsel.

Every Dog found running about Camp at large shall be shot at the discretion of the Capt. —

The emigrants traveled in covered wagons, popularly known as prairie schooners because their billowing tops resembled ships as they traveled through a sea of grass. The wagons were smaller and lighter than the eastern Conestoga wagon, but they could carry as much as a ton and a half and were better equipped to traverse muddy streams and sloughs. In spite of its advantages, the prairie schooner had a cramped interior and was considered a rough ride. Most people chose to walk, and they generally ate and slept outside.

The wagons were normally pulled by oxen, adult male cattle of any breed that have been castrated and trained to work as draft animals. Mules were occasionally used, but it was widely known that oxen can pull longer and harder than horses or mules and were better able than other animals to find forage. The trip usually began with at least four yoke of oxen with the expectation that some would become lame, sick, or lost during the journey. Advice on necessary equipment including wagons, animals, food, utensils, clothing, and weaponry came from frontiersmen, letters from those who had previously traveled the trail, newspapers, and magazines. Families generally brought horses, sheep, and cattle and a limited number of personal belongings. The Oregon Emigrating Company, one of the companies that took the Meek Cutoff, with 100 men and 193 women and children, brought with them 624 cattle, 398 oxen, 74 horses and mules, and 66 wagons. Those emigrants subject to the 1845 Oregon

Emigrating Company Constitution were permitted no more than thirty-three head of cattle for each driver. Each family was urged to bring a stove, tent, cooking fixtures, water kegs, tools, bedding, guns, ammunition, and food. One emigrant advised bringing two hundred pounds of flour, seventy-five pounds of bacon, ten pounds of rice, five pounds of coffee, twenty-five pounds of sugar, and appropriate amounts of tea, dried fruit, salt, cornmeal, vinegar, medicines, and, of course, clothing.

THE LOST WAGON TRAIN OF 1845

In early May 1845, several hundred wagons, as many as twenty-five hundred emigrants, and thousands of animals departed Independence and St. Joseph, Missouri, bound for Oregon. Group leaders included diarist Samuel Parker; Samuel Hancock, who was to write invaluable reminiscences; Solomon Tetherow; and W. G. T'Vault. Brief biographies of Hancock and Parker can be found on pp. 14–15. Solomon Tetherow was a notable hunter and trapper. After he arrived in Oregon, he farmed land in the Willamette Valley. W. G. T'Vault, while apparently not a named wagon train captain, after arrival in Oregon became the editor of the *Oregon Spectator*, the first newspaper published west of the Missouri River. T'Vault, a lawyer, served as a member of the Provisional Legislature of Oregon in 1846 and was elected speaker of the House of the Oregon Territorial Legislature in 1858.

Solomon Tetherow

Also part of the 1845 journey was Joel Palmer, an unusual emigrant. While serving in the Indiana State Legislature in 1844, he read a pamphlet describing the Oregon Territory. He was so enthusiastic about the prospects, he told his family that he wanted to visit the area and then joined the 1845 emigrants as a "tourist." The experience confirmed his excitement about the Oregon Territory. He gathered his family and in 1847 led the emigration of that year, eventually settling in Dayton, Oregon. Palmer's journal, a guide for emigrants, was used for years to prepare settlers for the journey west.

At the outset high excitement and enthusiasm characterized the prospective travelers, but various disagreements soon separated the 1845 emigrant companies into new groupings. Keith Clark and Lowell Tiller note that "every company was composed of strong-willed, vociferous pioneers who were not slow to criticize those who held positions of leadership." The organizing and reorganizing continued throughout the journey. In fact, Clark and Tiller conclude that so much shifting took place that it was "difficult to determine leadership and position of the various wagon groups on the long trail across the continent."

The crossing from Missouri to the Snake River at Fort Boise was relatively uneventful. Over the years, reports had drifted back to Missouri by letters and firsthand communications from travelers who returned from the West. The 1845 emigrants were certainly aware of at least some of the difficulties that lay ahead. They experienced Indian scares, buffalo stampedes, and cattle thievery, but those were not unusual or unexpected events.

Stephen Meek, a respected fur trader, trapper, and successful leader of an earlier Oregon expedition, was elected pilot of the Stephens-Palmer-

Stephen Meek

Barlow Company, a small part of the overall train. Meek, born in Virginia on July 4, 1805, left home at age twenty and worked for the Rocky Mountain Fur Company. In 1835, he came to the Oregon country and was employed by the Hudson's Bay Company trapping in the Pacific Northwest. Meek began guiding emigrant parties in 1842, and in 1845 he offered his services to part of the 1845 emigration. Several companies agreed to pay Meek $250, with $30 in advance and the remainder when the companies arrived in the Oregon country at Fort Vancouver, on the Columbia River near present-day Portland.

While Meek's services ended at Fort Hall in present-day southeastern Idaho, the reasons for his termination are unclear. According to Clark and Tiller, "Either the companies were dissatisfied with his piloting, the original agreement had been to lead them this far, or the original group was so splintered that a pilot's service were hopeless. It is of interest to note that in 1846 Meek sued Presley Welch for $130 of the pilotage fee and was awarded $66. The fact that he was not paid in full may signify that he left the companies on his own initiative."

Meek then rode ahead with his wife, whom he had met and married just prior to departure from Missouri, to Fort Boise. Apparently, as he traveled west, he attempted to persuade the emigrants with whom he came in contact to follow him on a new allegedly shorter and easier route to The Dalles. The last section of the Oregon Trail, then only a few years old, ran from Fort Boise across the Blue Mountains and finally to The Dalles. It was difficult, time consuming, and traversed hostile Indian country. In fact, the superintendent at Fort Boise, James Craigie, warned the emigrants of potential problems with the Walla Walla and Cayuse Indians on the trail ahead. Several years earlier, Meek had trapped the Malheur River headwaters in what is now eastern Oregon and apparently felt certain that his proposed shortcut up the Malheur River, across an open area to the Deschutes River, and then down the Deschutes to The Dalles, was a better route.

Several companies arrived at Fort Boise near the present-day Oregon-Idaho state line in mid-August, where they were greeted by Meek. Fort Boise, built by the Hudson's Bay Company in 1838, was a small quadrangular structure roughly one hundred feet on each side surrounded with a stockade of poles fifteen feet high. While not a prepossessing structure, it was no doubt a welcome sight to the tired pioneers. Meek persuaded some twelve hundred emigrants driving about two hundred wagons and two thousand head of loose livestock to join him on his proposed shortcut. On August 24, 1845, at what is now Vale, Oregon, the train divided. Meek's group turned west up the Malheur River. The remaining emigrants kept to the established trail northwest across the Blue Mountains.

In his reminiscences, emigrant W. A. Goulder writes:

On reaching old Fort Boise, late in the afternoon of a bright day in September [August], 1845, our company went into camp on the right bank of the Snake River, just below the fort. The Hudson Bay Company's agent at that place was Mr. Payette, after whom the Payette River had been named. Besides the agent and his people, there were several hundred Indians in the bottom near the place where we were encamped for the night. Stephen Meek, a brother of the somewhat renowned Joseph L. Meek, had overtaken us as we were journeying down the Boise Valley. Meek was accompanied by his young wife whom he had married somewhere on the road, and also by a young man, Nathan Olney, who afterwards became prominent in the history of Oregon. From Fort Boise westward, the route heretofore taken by the immigrants was the old Hudson Bay route by the way of Burnt River and the Grande Rounde Valley, and across the Blue Mountains, to the waters of the Umatilla River. It had been made known to us that the Walla Walla and Cayuse Indians, who then inhabited the country west of the Blue Mountains, the region through which the above-named route lay, were somewhat disposed to be unfriendly to the whites, and that they had threatened to make themselves troublesome to immigrants passing through the country. At Fort Boise, Meek told us that we could avoid all trouble and danger by taking a

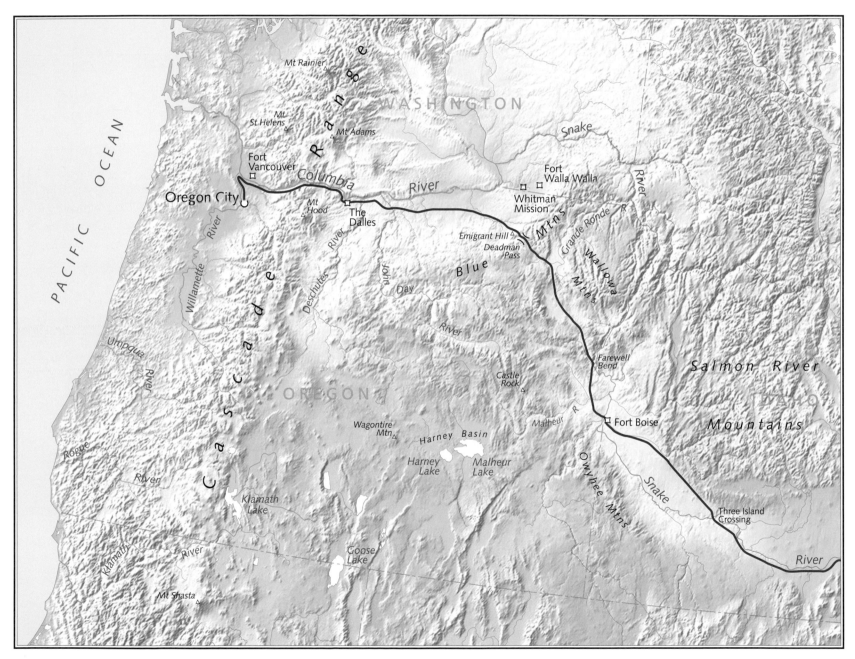

MAP 2 Oregon Trail, from Fort Boise to Oregon City

route over which he could guide us from Fort Boise to The Dalles of the Columbia. With the assistance of Olney, Meek made a crude map of the country, showing a route up the Malheur River and across low intervening ridges to the Des Chutes, and thence to The Dalles. This route, he said, would give the Cayuse and Walla Walla country a wide berth and enable us to avoid all contact with the supposedly hostile Indians.

Another emigrant, William Barlow, a member of the 1845 train, offered a similar explanation in his reminiscence:

We had hired Steve Meek, brother of Joe Meek, to pilot the emigrants clear through to The Dalles, for one dollar a wagon and board. He said he knew every trail and camping ground from Fort Laramie to Vancouver, west of the Cascade mountains. But he proved himself to be a reckless humbug from start to finish. All he had in view was to get the money and a white woman for a wife before he got through. He got the wife and part of the money. He and his company then went on and made a stand at the mouth of the Malheur river, which empties into the Snake River, where, he said, he could make a cut-off that would take them to The Dalles before we could get to the Grande Ronde Valley. This route, he said would give them plenty of wood, water and grass all the way, and there would be no Blue Mountain to cross, which he described as almost impassable.

The late summer is traditionally the driest time of year in the high desert of eastern Oregon, with an annual precipitation of approximately ten inches. The desert is largely covered with sagebrush but has open patches of basalt rock with many rocky peaks and valleys and an occasional timbered area. There are few spots with potable surface water. Many travelers, then and now, describe it as a formidable country, but many also find its ruggedness beautiful. Meek had the misfortune of proposing a shortcut during a time of extreme drought. A study of tree rings suggests that 1839 to 1854 was a particularly dry period in that area's weather history. In *The Brazen Overlanders of 1845* Donna Wojcik notes that tree ring studies show the year 1833 at some 25 percent below normal precipitation and then declining to 41 percent below normal in 1845.

Meek led his group up the Malheur River until they were forced by the terrain to leave the river bottom and travel over dusty, rocky hills with little or no access to water. Hiking across this stark land, the members of our Meek Research Expedition could appreciate the dreariness and the discouragement that must have characterized each difficult day. The parties were spread out with the lead wagons often several days in advance of the stragglers. The train crossed part of the Stinkingwater Mountains and

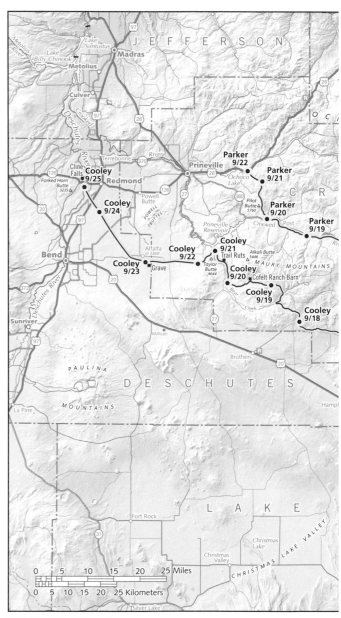

MAP 3 Meek Trail Overview

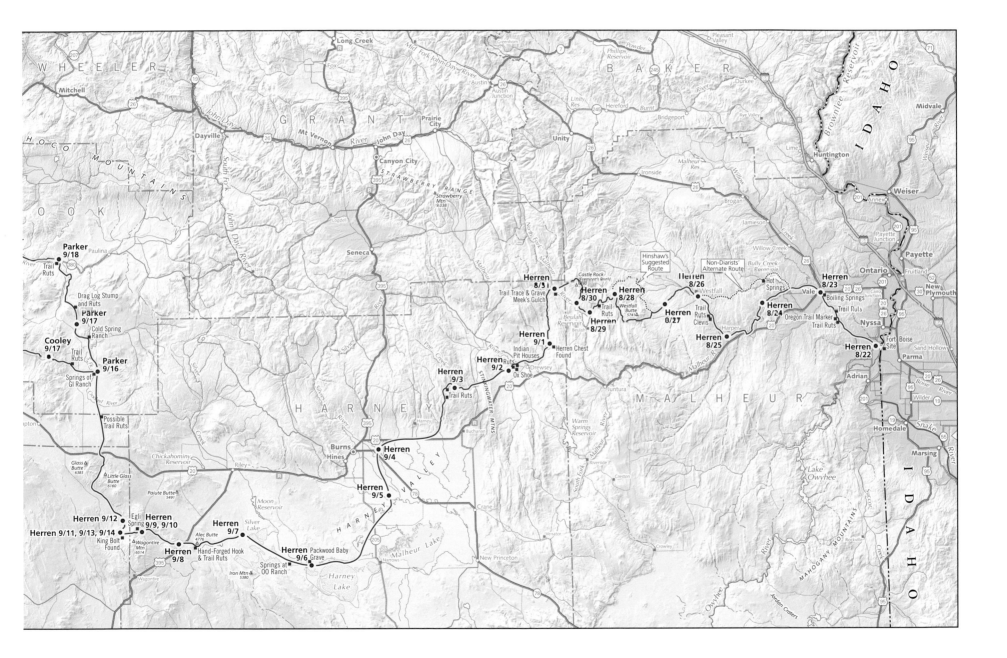

Parker
9/18

Trail
Ruts

Drag Log Stump
and Ruts

Parker
9/17   Cold Spring
                   Ranch

Cooley
9/17   Trail
                   Ruts

Parker
9/16

Springs of
GI Ranch

Possible
Trail Ruts

Glass △
Butte
6385   Little Glass
                  Butte
                  6160

Paiute Butte △
5491

Herren 9/12   Egli   Herren
                    Spring 9/9, 9/10
Herren 9/11, 9/13, 9/14

King Bolt
Found   Wagontire
                    Mtn △   Herren   Hand-Forged Hook
                    6514   9/8   & Trail Ruts

Wagontire

Alec Butte
4776   Herren
                             9/7   Silver
                                             Lake

Moon
Reservoir

Iron Mtn △
5380   Springs at   Herren   Packwood Baby
                 00 Ranch   9/6   Grave

Harney
Lake

Herren
8/31
                Trail Trace & Grave
                Meek's Gulch

Herren   Herren
8/30   8/28

Herren   Westfall
9/1   Trail   Butte
                Ruts   5741 △

Herren
8/29
Herren
8/27

Herren   Herren
9/2   Ruts   Herren Chest
                Ox Shoe   Found

Herren   Indian
9/3   Pit Houses

                Trail Ruts

Castle Rock
Fremont's Peak
4180

Hinshaw's
Suggested
Route

Non-Diarists'
Alternate Route

Herren
8/26   Westfall   Hot
                               Springs

Herren
8/27   Trail
                Ruts
                Clevis

Herren
8/25

Herren
8/23

Boiling Springs

Herren
8/24   Oregon Trail Marker
                Trail Ruts

Herren
8/22

Burns
Hines   Herren
                9/4

Herren
9/5

then descended into the Harney Valley. The trail improved. It leveled out and grass and water became abundant. At this point, Meek apparently became confused; he did not realize that he had traveled forty to fifty miles south of an east-west line running from Vale to Bend or Redmond, Oregon. He may have believed that he was on the Crooked River in the Deschutes watershed. In fact, the emigrants were on the Silvies River, which flows south into Malheur Lake. Meek then led the train toward Harney Lake at the western end of the Harney Valley and then to Silver Lake, now, and possibly then, a dry lakebed. As they traveled, it became apparent to the train's leaders that Meek was lost. The lush valley turned to desert. The feelings at this time were well described in Goulder's reminiscence:

> We traveled up the Malheur several days, and then, crossing over some very steep hills, entered a region of arid sage plains, marshes, and small lakes. The ground becoming soft and spongy, with no prospect of improvement, so far as we could see, in front, we were obliged to counter-march upon our trail in order to regain the higher ground we had left. This changed the direction in which we had been traveling and entirely destroyed what little confidence we had left in the competence of our guide. It had been becoming more and more evident to us that Meek had no more knowledge of the country through which we were passing than we had

ourselves, and that, like us, he was seeing it for the first time.

> We had entered upon this new and untrodden route at a time when our oxen were already worn down and foot-sore by the long trip, thus far, across the plains, and when we were all tired and several of the company sick from exposure, privation, and fatigue.

The train continued west and finally the lead wagons came in sight of Wagontire Mountain.

When they arrived at that low-lying mound, the emigrants were lost, starving, and essentially without water. Some of them threatened to hang Meek, but wiser heads prevailed. After encamping at Wagontire Mountain for several days, with scouts searching for water in all directions, a possible source was seen from a high location northwest of the encampment. An all-night race to water, on what is now the GI Ranch, some fifteen miles north of Glass Butte, prevented a complete disaster.

After a short rest, the wagons split, with some traveling north to the Crooked River and then down that river to the Deschutes. The others went due west, over Hampton Butte, along the south side of the Maury Mountains, across Alkali Butte and then across the desert floor to Cline Falls on the Deschutes River, just west of Redmond, Oregon. Reasons for the split are unknown, but it is likely the train's leaders disagreed about the safest and most rapid route to The Dalles.

The two sections of the Meek Cutoff train met at Sagebrush Springs, some four miles south of Madras, Oregon, on September 27, 1845. The emigrants were exhausted and short of food. Many were ill. Samuel Parker's diary noted that six emigrants died at the springs. From there the weakened emigrants traveled through the Hay Creek Valley to Trout Creek to the summit of Shaniko Flat and then to the Deschutes River and the canyon at the present day site of Sherars Bridge. The crossing of the Deschutes River at Sherars Bridge, widely documented in diaries and reminiscences, was as traumatic as any event during the journey. Goulder, in his Reminiscences, wrote:

> The point at which we struck the Des Chutes River presented the most unfavorable place for crossing the stream that could well be imagined. The river is, at that point, about four rods wide, flowing between perpendicular walls of basalt, the water very deep and the current very rapid. No one, except the Indians, had ever thought of crossing the stream at that point.

But with the assistance of helpful Indians, probably Paiutes, the emigrants dragged and pulled their wagons and animals across the river. From Sherars Bridge, the emigrants began straggling into The Dalles on October 7. After resting at The Dalles, some of the emigrants rafted down the dangerous rapid-filled Columbia River to its confluence with

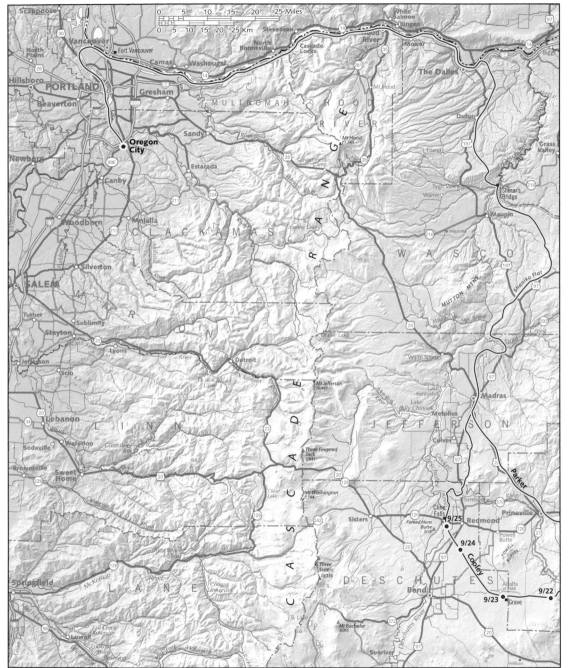

MAP 4 Route of the two Meek parties from Cline Falls and the Crooked River to The Dalles and to Oregon City

the Willamette and then traveled up the fertile Willamette Valley to Oregon City. I suspect that others struggled over either the north or south side of Mt. Hood to the Willamette Valley.

Clark and Tiller suggest that a minimum of twenty-four emigrants died on the Cutoff as the train traveled from Vale to The Dalles. Joel Palmer wrote that some twenty additional emigrants died at The Dalles from exhaustion and malnutrition. Undoubtedly, others died in the following months as a result of the harrowing trek across eastern Oregon.

In his autobiography, which describes the remarkable life of a true "mountain man," Stephen Meek summarizes his 1845 year in two paragraphs:

> In March 1845, I went to New Orleans and then up the river to St. Louis, where I got letters of recommendation from Fitzpatrick, Wm. Sublette and Rob. Campbell, which secured me a position as guide to the immense emigrant train of 480 wagons then preparing to go to Oregon. We started on the 11th of May, 1845, on which day I first saw Elizabeth Schoonover, whom I married a week later.
>
> Arriving at Fort Hall, one-third of the train … went to California. … The remainder, I conducted safely to Oregon.

The summary phrase "conducted safely to Oregon" strikes one as a flagrant misstatement. Either

Meek's memory of the travails of the Lost Wagon Train failed him or, more likely, he wanted to keep his legacy free of the disastrous 1845 experience.

The Meek train was famous, not only for the hardships suffered by the emigrants, but also because members of the train allegedly discovered, and then were unable to relocate, a gold lode, the legendary Blue Bucket discovery. Searching for and speculating on the location of this gold has attracted the attention of hundreds of people during the intervening 168 years, and was of great interest to members of our expedition. It was the part of the story that first caught my attention when I was a small boy.

The suffering experienced on the Meek Cutoff led to many of the deaths that occurred as the wagons struggled into The Dalles and later, the Willamette Valley. Most certainly, the travails experienced during the most difficult part of the journey produced the stories of desperation, hardship, and resolve that are now legend in Oregon history.

THE DIARIES, DIARISTS, AND REMINISCENCES

Reading and appreciating the descriptive words of the five known diarists who traveled the Meek Cutoff is absolutely essential to understanding the difficulties and desperation that faced the emigrants as they traveled west. The four published diarists are James Field, Jesse Harritt, John Herren, and Samuel Parker; a fifth diary, unpublished, by Eli Cooley was brought to my attention. The following summary biographies of the diarists were prepared by historian Steve Lent, a member of the Meek Research Expedition, from a variety of sources. The photographs are from the collection at the A. R. Bowman Memorial Museum in Prineville, Oregon.

Eli Cooley was born in Howard County, Missouri, in 1821. He was twenty-three years old when he made the trip west by wagon. After arriving in Oregon in 1845, he settled in the Willamette Valley near Woodburn, Oregon Territory. He married Lydia Bonney on October 18, 1849 in Woodburn. They had four children. Cooley died in Marion County, Oregon, on August 26, 1882.

James Field was born in 1823 in Port Chester, New York. It is believed that he never married. After taking the Meek Cutoff on the Oregon Trail, he settled in the Willamette Valley for a short while before heading to California in 1847. He returned home to New York and died in Port Chester, New York, on May 19, 1903.

Jesse Harritt was born in Indiana in 1818, came west in 1845, and settled in Polk County, where he farmed until his death on March 27, 1888. In 1846, he married Julia Lewis, the stepdaughter of James McNary, the captain of the wagon train in which Harritt traveled the Oregon Trail. Harritt was an elder in the Brethren Church and was a traveling minister for many years. Harritt's wife Julia died in Salem in 1908.

John Daniel Herren was born in Lexington, Kentucky, on September 30, 1799, and married Theodosha Robbins in 1822. After coming west on the Oregon Trail, the family settled in Marion County, Oregon Territory. They had ten children. Herren died on March 2, 1864, in Marion County. Theodosha died on September 15, 1881.

Samuel Parker was born in 1806. In 1828, he married Elizabeth Sutton, and they had ten children. In 1845, they left their home in Van Buren County, Iowa, and joined travelers on the Oregon Trail. Elizabeth, their infant son born on the trail, and a daughter died at the end of the journey. Parker arrived in the Willamette Valley in November 1845 and settled in Oregon City. In 1846, he married Rosetta Spears and they later moved to Marion County. He was elected to the Provisional Legislature of Oregon to represent the Champoeg District in the last session of that body before the territorial government was formed early in 1849. Parker served as president of the upper chamber of the council of the Oregon Territorial Legislature in 1851. In 1858, he returned to the legislature for the final session before statehood. Parker was elected to the Oregon House of Representatives in 1860 and served in the first session of the Oregon Legislative Assembly. He died in 1886.

Eli Casey Cooley (*front left*) and family, 1870

James Field

Jesse Harritt, ca. 1880

John Herren

Samuel Parker, ca. 1880

In addition to these five known diaries, there are several publications that provide important information about the Meek Cutoff and the emigrant experience generally. Reminiscences by W. A. Goulder and Samuel Hancock were especially valuable and have been cited throughout this book.

W. A. Goulder was an educated man. After arriving in Oregon City in December 1845, he taught school for several years, then moved to Idaho in 1861 and mined for a living. Later he served in the Idaho Legislature and also worked as an editor of the *Idaho Statesman.*

After arriving in Oregon, *Samuel Hancock* was involved with the Oregon Territory Indian Wars of 1848. Later he traveled to the gold diggings in California. Married in 1860, he settled on Whidbey Island, Washington.

The various wagon companies were led by persons whose names were associated with those companies, such as Parker, McNary, Riggs, Ownbey, and Tetherow. Except for Parker for part of the journey, the diarists were not captains of their companies. Ownbey's company included Meek as well as Herren, Hancock, and Goulder, whose reminiscences are an important part of the story.

The location of the various diarists as discussed later in this book is fully described in Clark and Tiller's *Terrible Trail: The Meek Cutoff, 1845.* As noted above, Herren traveled with Ownbey. (Herren's diary, located in 1968, was unknown to Clark and Tiller when their book was published in 1966.) The companies of Parker, McNary, and Riggs merged east of Fort Boise. Riggs was elected captain of the forty-wagon group. Diarists Field, Harritt, and Parker were with the Riggs party. Clark and Tiller note that various other sections, including a company captained by Tetherow, none with a known diarist, tended to follow behind Riggs. We were unable to determine Cooley's traveling companions. *For clarity and simplicity, I will refer to the wagon companies and their location only by the diarists' names.*

THE MEEK RESEARCH EXPEDITION

Although expedition members met on several occasions prior to starting our field research, the day-to-day journey began on August 22, 2006, when our party met in Ontario, Oregon, near the Idaho border. The following day, 161 years after some of the emigrants traveled from Fort Boise on the Idaho side of the Snake River sixteen miles to the hot springs at Vale, Oregon, we started to repeat that trek.

We spent approximately two weeks in 2006 and in each of the following three years defining parts of Meek's Cutoff Trail. In 2009, several expedition members accompanied me as we flew over the trail by helicopter. We flew east with the afternoon sun setting behind us and flew west the following morning with the sun again behind us. Parts of the trail were easier to locate with the sun at our back. Following the helicopter trip in 2009, we spent several days reinvestigating the trail and several days again during the summer of 2010 on the same mission. At the end of most days, we reviewed our findings following dinner and also planned the next days' exploration. We also, almost always, read aloud the diary entries for each day.

The expedition initially based its exploration on the trail shown on a 1995 Bureau of Land Management map. We understood that this trail was essentially the route suggested by Del Hinshaw. In 1992, Bob Boyd and Hinshaw had spent several weeks following sections of that route. Boyd and Hinshaw found wagon parts, drag logs, and other pioneer remnants, which enabled them to locate some parts of the trail with accuracy. Shortly after an exhibit at the High Desert Museum in Bend, Oregon, titled "Wandering Wagons: Meek's Lost Emigrants of 1845," Steve Lent traced much of the Meek Cutoff from the GI Ranch, approximately a hundred miles east of Bend, to the Deschutes River and on to The Dalles.

Our expedition needed a knowledgeable mapping expert so that we could accurately locate our specific findings. Art McEldowney provided those skills. Art's mapping, coupled with Del Hinshaw's original maps and our own discoveries, were used by me, by Jim Meacham at the University of Oregon's Cartography Department, and by Stuart Allan of Allan Cartography to locate the trail with as much accuracy as we could bring to the project.

John Herren's trail descriptions were relatively simple and complete and I believe we located his route accurately. The routes of the other diarists, particularly Eli Cooley and Samuel Parker, were more difficult to determine. Herren's diary was obviously used by Del Hinshaw as the basis for his location of the trail. While our trail definition occasionally differs from Hinshaw's, we generally tended to agree with his mapping.

Even though the diarists were uncertain of their location, their description of the terrain and their mileage numbers gave us clues about the trail and campsites. As noted earlier, the diarists did not travel together. The train, with as many as two hundred wagons, traveled in sections, often separated by a day or more. Various wagon groupings traveled at different speeds and often took different routes. Sometimes the companies split, joined other companies, or regrouped. Most sections of the train traveled without a diarist. All of the known diarists recorded a particular path of travel but the sections with no diarist may, and sometimes did, travel a different route. The image of two hundred wagons moving together across the desert was a dramatic fiction. The dust created by just the three vehicles we used was often very unpleasant. Imagine the dust created by two hundred wagons and accompanying animals traveling very slowly in intense heat over very dry terrain. Moreover, a single campsite for some twelve hundred people and thousands of animals obviously would have presented enormous hygiene problems. Smaller separate groupings also afforded more grass for animals and water for both humans and animals.

Camp locations tend to correspond to diary descriptions and are the expedition's best guesses. The location of artifacts, tree stumps, wagon parts, wagon ruts, diarists' mileage figures, as well as occasional help from local history buffs all provided useful input.

The suggested location of some segments of the trail itself is sometime no better than an estimate. Subsequent activity such as ranching, farming, U.S. Army road activity, commercial wagon freight traffic, and more than 168 years of weather can destroy all evidence of ruts or campsites. Still, I feel confident that our locations of the trail and of most of the campsites represent the likely course of travel and are reasonably accurate. We are well aware that discovery of additional diaries or new on-the-ground findings may lead to further insights.

Old trail ruts are often very difficult to identify many decades after the emigrants' wagons created them. Ruts begin to form when wagons, rolling over the ground, compact the soil. During rainy periods the runoff tends to create a depression or a ditch and that is usually the rut remnant we walked. Clearly, it is much easier to find and follow ruts when they are going up or down hills because of water runoff. The trail or rut can be quite evident when one is in or standing near it, but can be difficult to photograph because the image may not show the depression and new vegetation tends to obscure the ruts. Ruts are most visible early or late in the day when light falls sideways and creates shadows.

Some of the ruts, wagon parts, and other evidence of Meek's route from Vale to the Harney Valley could be associated with the Elijah Elliott party of 1853 and possibly with a small group led by William M. Macy in 1854. In 1853, Elliott led a wagon train of emigrants across eastern Oregon. It was his intention to lead a group of emigrants on Meek's route, leaving it at an appropriate point and crossing the Cascade Range to the upper Willamette Valley.

While Elliott purportedly followed the Meek Trail from Vale to the Harney Valley, entries of the party's lone diarist, Andrew S. McClure, do not add much usable description to the information provided by the five diarists who took the 1845 Meek Cutoff. McClure's most interesting observations concerned Elliott's travel south around Malheur and Harney Lakes. The diarists of the Meek party clearly traveled around the north side of the lakes. Some historians have argued that Meek and some members of the 1845 party went south around the lakes, but we found no evidence of such a trail.

The lead wagons were usually preceded by out-riders or scouts who attempted to determine the best route for the wagon train. During daylight hours, they occasionally marked the trail with piles of rock; at night, the outriders set fires. Since the wagons had a high center of gravity, they tended to be somewhat top heavy. The outriders tried to find as straight and as level a trail as possible. The route through eastern Oregon was highly challenging.

EASTERN OREGON IN 1845

THIS MAP OF PART OF THE OREGON TERRITORY is a portion of a larger map published in an 1845 book by Robert Greenhow, who was considered an authority on the Northwest Coast. Clearly, eastern Oregon was largely unknown territory in 1845. Few of the rivers or mountains shown on the map are located with accuracy. While there is no evidence that Stephen Meek or other 1845 emigrants had knowledge of this map or any other map of the area, the map is evidence that the emigrants were traveling into an unknown place—"terra incognita."

MAP 5 A portion of 1845 "Map of the Western and Middle Portion of North America" prepared by George H. Ring-gold. From Robert Greenhow, *The History of Oregon and California, and the Other Territories on the North-West Coast of North America* (1845). Reproduced courtesy of the Pacific Northwest Archives, Suzzallo Library, University of Washington.

GUIDELINES FOR THE MODERN-DAY EXPLORER

ONE HUNDRED YEARS AGO, AN ADVENTURER who wanted to explore eastern Oregon simply rode his horse and wagon into the desert. Not today. Today's explorer in the American West needs to consider the following:

1. While public lands are open to everyone, when conducting formal research it may be helpful, although not required, to request a Bureau of Land Management Cultural Resources Permit. In any case, the researcher should check with the local BLM office for seasonal restrictions regarding fire, muddy roads, or other conditions.

2. Collecting artifacts is not permitted on public lands. Federal environmental laws prohibit removing artifacts. Items can be lifted, examined, and photographed, but then must be replaced where found.

3. The possibility of fires, often ignited by sagebrush or grass caught in a vehicle's catalytic converter, is a constant worry. All vehicles on public lands should carry fire-fighting equipment. Regulations require that builders of campfires carry a shovel and one gallon of water. Damage to private ranchlands opens the door to legal action.

4. While federal regulations do not require backup tools and equipment, common sense strongly suggests spare tires, cell phones, two-way radios, and extra food and water among other items. After summer thunderstorms, some "roads" in eastern Oregon are impassable for days.

5. Much of eastern Oregon now consists of private land holdings, most often ranches, interspersed with federal and state lands. Private-property trespassing laws are enforced, occasionally with a gun. Permission to enter and explore is generally required and not always granted. Meek Research Expedition members distributed a handout that was useful in explaining our venture to landowners.

In addition to these general guidelines, in the case of the Meek Research Expedition the expedition leader was in charge of making motel and hotel reservations, locating gas stations, providing lunch supplies of food, water, ice, and beverages, and funding. The leader reserved tables for breakfasts and dinners and a private room every evening to review the day's activities and discuss plans for the following day.

ODOMETERS

Roadometer

READERS SHOULD KEEP IN MIND THAT THERE may be substantial inaccuracies in the mileage figures reported in the pioneer diaries. The primitive odometers sometimes malfunctioned, particularly as the wagons traveled over the rocky, inhospitable Meek route. Moreover, the topography of the land usually did not permit straight-line travel. The line of travel from Westfall to the Beulah Reservoir was particularly uneven, broken by ridges, hills, ravines, and a variety of stony outcroppings. Often it was a struggle to fit the reported mileage to the written description of each day's travel.

Norman E. Wright, professor emeritus of Computer Science at Brigham Young University, is probably the country's most knowledgeable historian of odometers from ancient history to and through the nineteenth century. At my request, Dr. Wright wrote a short history of the odometer in which he emphasized its importance to nineteenth-century American pioneers. His preface states the problem:

> During the early history of Tennessee, if you had asked a rural farmer, "How far is it to Knoxville?", his answer might have been, "It's twelve sees from here." He would have meant:

> Go straight down this road as far as you can see. At that point, look again, straight down the road as far as you can see. Repeat this process twelve times and you will be in Knoxville.

Those instructions may have gotten you to Knoxville, but they would not have told you how far it was nor the time required to get there. A more precise and useful answer to the question of the distance to Knoxville would require a measured, numeric value and not just a series of visual reference points.

For thousands of years, the wheel has been used to measure distance. In a letter to me, Dr. Wright noted that "the circumference of a wheel, multiplied by the number of times it rotates while traveling from point to point, is a relatively accurate measure of the distance between them." The devices that count wheel rotations are known as hodometers, odometers, viameters, waywisers, and roadometers.

Thomas Jefferson used an odometer to measure the distance from Philadelphia to Monticello. In the early nineteenth century, the U.S. Army's Topographical Engineers used odometers to measure and map various areas of the United States.

Perhaps the most publicized use of the odometer in the pioneer era occurred in 1847, when Mormon pioneers used two wooden odometers to measure their travels to the Great Salt Lake. As Dr. Wright explains, "A gear-counting mechanism, mounted on the side of a wagon, was activated by a threaded shaft linked to a wheel's rotation." Similar devices were attached to the wagons of the diarists traveling the 1845 wagon train.

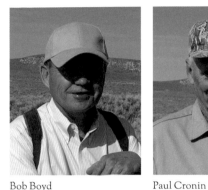

Bob Boyd   Paul Cronin   Margi Heater   Steve Lent   Art McEldowney   Jane McEldowney

MEEK RESEARCH EXPEDITION MEMBERS

Since 1972 *Bob Boyd* has been a middle school teacher in Bend, Oregon, where his classes include studies of the American West. A lifetime of traveling the West, collecting pieces of its past, and visiting museums, led to a volunteer job at the High Desert Museum in Bend when it opened in 1982. His role grew over time, and for many years he served as curator of Western History at the museum, retiring in 2012. Bob has an intimate knowledge of the High Desert landscape and its people. In 1993, he researched and produced a High Desert Museum exhibit entitled *Wandering Wagons: Meek's Lost Emigrants of 1845*. The exhibit required two years of research and travel along parts of the route.

Paul Cronin was born in "Whiskey Flats," near Burns, Oregon. He grew up and still lives in Drewsey, Oregon, which has a current population of nineteen. Paul's education began in a one-room schoolhouse for elementary school where he was the only student in his class all eight years. Paul served in the U.S. Navy as a machinist's mate on the USS *Midway*, and he later worked for the U.S.

Forest Service as a cat skinner. He has been an assistant office manager and a roving relief manager for a finance company, an employee of sawmill and plywood plants, an insurance agent, and a range technician for the BLM. Paul is highly skilled with a metal detector and in retirement actively prospects Oregon and Nevada creeks and rivers for gold.

Margi Heater was born and raised on an Oregon ranch, and her family still owns their original land grant property. After a career in the corporate world, she returned to Bend and began volunteering at the High Desert Museum in Bend in 1998. Margi was the museum's chairman of the board in 2007 and 2008. Her great-great-grandparents, Christopher and Nancy Cooley, came to Oregon with Meek in 1845. Christopher's brother Eli's unpublished diary, brought to my attention by Margi, was of great help to this expedition. Margi is highly skilled with a metal detector, and has worked over the years on historical-trail discovery.

Steve Lent is a native of Crook County, Oregon. Most of his career was with the Ochoco National Forest and the Bureau of Land Management. After

retirement, Steve became the assistant director of the A. R. Bowman Memorial Museum in Prineville. In that capacity, he has thoroughly studied the portion of the trail running from the GI Ranch to Bend. He has led numerous tours visiting significant points of interest on the western section of the Meek Trail and has written several publications that locate and describe the trail. Steve has also authored books on Crook and Wheeler counties and has received a commendation award from the National Association of State and Local History. He is a member of Western Writers of America.

Art McEldowney, a native Oregonian, spent most of his working life in the foreign service of the U.S. Department of State, specializing in diplomatic telecommunications. Art is the owner of BLN Digital Media, providing digital photography services, map and compass training, GPS, and survival techniques. Art has superb technical skills. He has traveled most of the high desert of eastern Oregon.

Jane McEldowney has had a distinguished career as a registered nurse. She is the owner of Called to Nursing, providing camp-nurse consulting and

Ellen Morris Bishop   Brooks Ragen   Suzanne Ragen   Lee Schaefer   Lynne Schaefer   Del Hinshaw

public speaking, with in-character presentations of Florence Nightingale. She served as our medical advisor and assisted with mapping.

Ellen Morris Bishop, Ph.D., is a geologist, professional photographer, environmental advocate, and teacher. Ellen wrote *In Search of Ancient Oregon: A Geologic and Natural History,* which was published by Timber Press in 2003 and later released in paperback. She is a visiting professor of geology and environmental studies and teaches photography at Whitman College, Walla Walla, Washington.

Brooks Ragen, the author, is a native Oregonian, and has spent his working life in the investment business in New York and Seattle. He has worked as a security analyst, a branch manager, corporate finance officer, and co-founder and manager of two investment firms. He is a member of the Oregon State Bar Association. Brooks is past president of many Seattle civic organizations and has served on several corporate boards. Oregon pioneer history, and especially the story of the Meek Cutoff, has been a lifelong interest.

Suzanne Ragen was born in Czechoslovakia and came to the United States in 1939. She is a long-time docent with the Seattle Art Museum. She has willingly, and sometimes enthusiastically, accompanied her husband on various adventures. Susie was responsible for our meals on the trail.

Lee Schaefer served in the U.S. Navy in the South Pacific in World War II. After the war, he became a television-broadcast cameraman and video technician and filmed a variety of professional and college sporting events including the Goodwill Games in Seattle and Summer Olympic Games in Atlanta and Australia. Lee is an accomplished photographer, with still photographs published in a wide variety of publications. In retirement at Sunriver, Oregon, Lee provides photography and video services, on a volunteer basis, for the High Desert Museum in Bend.

Lynne Schaefer has held a wide variety of jobs, mostly in journalism. Her garden, travel, and human-interest articles have been published in many regional magazines. Her book, *A Traveler's Guide to Historic California,* was published in 2002. Lynne also volunteers at the High Desert Museum in Bend.

In preparing for *Wandering Wagons: Meek's Lost Emigrants of 1845,* the exhibit that opened at the High Desert Museum in 1993, museum curator Bob Boyd interviewed *Delmar Hinshaw.* Hinshaw, although he died in 1997 at age eighty-one, has been, in absentia, a real member of our group. All of us referred to Del by his first name as though he were with us. Highlights from a short biography prepared by expedition member Steve Lent follow:

Del was born in Mt. Vernon, Oregon, and grew up hearing stories of the Meek Trail from his grandparents. Del's great-grandfather Isaac Hinshaw arrived in the Oregon country with Marcus Whitman in 1843. Isaac later returned east to meet up with his brothers. Then he and his brothers followed Meek to the Oregon country in 1845. Incidentally, the Hinshaw covered wagon is now displayed at the Oregon Historical Society in Portland, Oregon. Del was one of the founders of the Mount Hood Stage Bus Line and was associated with that business for twenty-seven years. Steve Lent noted:

Del began researching and tracing the Meek Trail in the mid 1930's but his serious work began in 1941. He . . . located and mapped the Trail as well as located 39 graves between Vale and The Dalles. . . . Over the years Del . . . collected several diaries written by participants on the Lost Wagon Train. The information in the diaries, along with other research and Del's knowledge of the land, allowed him to map the location of the Trail, campsites, and graves. Del used his knowledge of the land to assist Tiller and Clark in their research on the Meek Trail. Although the three researchers disagree on some points relating to the Trail and its story they remained friends.

All of us on this expedition acknowledge an enormous debt to Del Hinshaw. While specific discoveries have occasionally forced us to revise his routings, his work has served as the basis for much of our travels. Our various discoveries have generally confirmed his findings.

THE GOLD

One of the most intriguing parts of the Meek Cutoff story involves a purported discovery of gold nuggets that became known as the Blue Bucket gold. While none of the known diaries from the 1845 wagon train mention such a discovery, interest in the Blue Bucket gold developed soon after the 1845 emigrants arrived in the Willamette Valley. An expedition

undertaken in 1858 to find the Blue Bucket site found nothing. Other parties searched in 1860, 1861, and 1863, but none located it. The search continued sporadically through the last century. Leah Collins Menefee and Lowell Tiller discuss some of the efforts by gold seekers to find the Blue Bucket lode in the sixth and last of a memorable series of articles titled "Cutoff Fever" published in the *Oregon Historical Quarterly* in 1976–78. The articles describe in detail the story of later emigrants who took the Meek Cutoff in the 1850s. In the spring 1978 summary article, the authors remark:

> The tale of the children in Meek's train who picked up shiny pebbles somewhere in eastern Oregon . . . has endured even until this day. It was never more than a chance discovery, but it fired many imaginations: Where men once sought the location of the blue bucket nuggets on horseback, their successors now comb the country on trail bikes or with Jeeps and four-wheel drive motor vehicles.

While searching for the emigrants' purported gold discovery was not one of the major objectives of the Meek Research Expedition, we nonetheless remained alert to the possibility. Expedition member Paul Cronin, a genuine gold prospector, served as our eyes on this matter.

Why was the alleged discovery named the Blue

Bucket? In 1938, a Works Progress Administration employee, Andrew C. Sherbert, interviewed W. H. Hembree, a miner and the son and grandson of 1843 Oregon pioneers, for his personal and family history. In discussing the naming of the Blue Bucket discovery, Hembree stated:

> A wagon train which is supposed to have stumbled onto the rich gold deposit, was made up of a string of wagons the bodies of which were painted blue. In those days wagons had no hub nuts to hold a wheel in place on the axle. Wheels were held on the axle by what was called a linch pin, which were merely a pin or bolt, that slipped through a hole in the axle outside the hub of the wheel. Between the hub and pin was a washer which rubbed on the hub. To prevent wear, it was necessary to constantly daub the axle, at the point of friction, with tar, which the immigrants carried in buckets that hung on a hook at the rear of the wagon. The tar buckets of this particular wagon train were also painted blue. The train made a "dry camp" (no water in sight) one night on a meadow in a valley between two ridges of hills. Needing water for their horses, members of the train set out on foot, each in a different direction, to attempt to locate a small creek or pond nearby. Each carried one of the blue tar buckets, in which to carry water if any were found. One

member came upon a wet, cozy spot, where it appeared water was near the surface of the ground. He dug down, using the bucket as a spade, and upon raising the bucket found it filled with wet dirt containing nuggets of gold. And that was how the Blue Bucket mine was discovered.

I was privileged once to see a diary said to have been kept by a man whose name, I believe, was Warren. The man was a member of the "Blue Bucket" train. In the diary he kept a day by day log of the train's progress. By a series of calculations, based upon the mileages and directions given in the diary, I was able to reach a position which must have been in the vicinity of the fabulous mine. To further convince me that I actually did find the mine's exact location, in my search I one day stumbled onto a weathered portion of a wagon box, with unmistakable traces of blue paint still visible on its bleached boards. That the wagon box was of the wagon-train era, was evidenced by the foot that it was built like a scow, or flat boat, and was caulked with rags, fragments of which were still intact. Emigrant wagons were constructed in such manner to permit them to ford streams handily without damaging their contents.

Well, there's my story of the "Blue Bucket" mine. Many think the mine never existed. I think it did, however, I realize that my story would carry far more conviction were I able to

exhibit a few buckets of gold taken from it—regardless the color of the buckets.

As far as can be discovered, the first written description of the Blue Bucket discovery site was published in the *Portland Daily Bee* of February 6, 1869:

The first gold discovery in Oregon made by any American, if not by any person, was near the head of the Malheur River, on a small creek divided from the Malheur by a ridge. This stream ran south-west, and was supposed to be a branch of the Malheur, an error that caused much trouble and disappointment to prospectors eight or ten years later. Daniel Herron, a cousin of W. J. Herron of Salem, was looking for lost cattle while the company were in camp here, and picked up a piece of shining metal on the rocky bed of the creek, and carried it to camp as a curiosity. No one could tell what the metal was, and no one thought of its being gold. Another nugget was found and brought to Mr. Martin's wagon, who tested it by hammering it out on his wagon-tire; but not being able to tell its nature, it was thrown into the tool-chest and forgotten, and ultimately lost. After the gold discovery in California these incidents were remembered, and many parties went in search of the spot where the emigrants said this gold was found, but were misled by being told it was on a tributary of the Malheur.

Interviews, newspaper reports, and reminiscences quoting emigrants, their heirs, relatives, friends, and acquaintances appeared during the latter part of the nineteenth century and the early part of the twentieth century. Many attempted to describe the site of the discovery. The reports vary widely and are often in conflict, but some of the common themes are worth noting.

Most reports cite Herren family members as the discoverers. The Herrens were then traveling with the Tetherow party. There are conflicting stories regarding which of the Herren family members actually discovered the gold nuggets. In a March 7, 1922, letter to the *Oregonian*, W. H. Herren, a grandson of the 1845 diarist, wrote:

Several of the young men that had saddled horses scouted the country over and finally found a ridge that led to the summit of the mountain. They concluded that if they could once get their outfits up on this ridge they could make it over the mountains. By hitching ten and sometimes twelve yoke of oxen at a time to a wagon they finally succeeded in getting them up onto the divide.

There was no water on the divide so they had to make a dry camp. The captain of the company told all of the young people who had saddle horses to take buckets and go hunt for water. My father, who was then 23 years old, and his sister, who afterwards became the wife of

William Wallace, took their old blue wooden buckets and started out to find water.

They finally found a dry creek bed which they followed until they found a place where a little water was seeping through the gravel, and while my father was digging for water his sister saw something bright and picked it up.

The account given me states that they found two good sized lumps or nuggets, and that there were many fine particles in the gravel. He was quite sure that it was gold at the time, and when he arrived at camp he showed it to some of the older men, who told him that if it was gold it would be mallable [sic]. So one of them took a hammer and hammered both pieces out flat into a saucer-shaped disc. . . .

When they reached the summit of the mountains they camped on a meadow, and while there some Warm Spring Indians came to their camp. One of the Indians could speak a little English. He told them that if some of them would go with him to a high ridge near by they could see down into the Deschutes and Crooked river valleys. He showed them some buttes that lay south of Prineville and said that they would find water there, but no water between there and the Deschutes. He also showed them what is now called pilot Butte and told them if they would steer straight for that butte they would find a place in the bend of the river where a man could cross it on a horse,

and for them to cross the Deschutes there and keep down the west side through by way of the Metolius and Tygh valley and that they would eventually reach The Dalles.

Many reports refer to a stream or creek running in a southwesterly direction, others to a stream running to the northeast. There are also repeated references to a "dry camp," a camp without water. Some accounts refer to a camp on a meadow between two ridges or a camp on a high ridge. Some writers state that from or near the site a big slide on the east slope of the Cascade Range was observable. One account refers to round stone huts seen near the discovery site. All reports state that it was in an area of juniper trees, not pine trees. Moreover, it was often reported that at or near the time of discovery the emigrants could see the Cascade Range. One account mentions that a helpful Indian led the pioneers to a nearby point and told them that water could be found near a butte, now known as Pilot Butte, which the Indian identified on the horizon. That sighting was reported to have occurred on the day of a "dry camp." One element of the purported discovery is not in dispute. Fred Lockley, in *Visionaries, Mountain Men & Empire Builders*, interviewed a son of Job McNemee, an emigrant on the Lost Train. The son reported that: "The immigrants were more interested in . . . securing food and water for their hungry and thirsty children and grass and water for their cattle than in gold, so no attention was paid to

the stream on which the nuggets had been found."

Two general locations are repeatedly suggested. If there really was a discovery, and if there is any credibility to the numerous stories and reports, the likely sites are creeks on springs near the so-called "headwaters of the Malheur" or the Hampton Butte-Maury Mountains area.

The emigrants reported seeing the Cascade Range around the time of the September 4th camp. In fact, the Cascade Range is not visible from that site. Steens Mountain, however, is visible and it is likely that the emigrants, obviously lost at the time, confused the mountain with the range. From the September 2nd camp near Drewsey, the emigrants traveled for two days in the Pine Creek drainage, a tributary or headwater of the Malheur. Their camp on the second day in the Pine Creek area was probably adjacent to Cow Creek near today's Highway 20, below the south end of the Pine Creek drainage. Possible sites would include locations from Cottonwood Creek to streams flowing into the Harney Valley from the west side of the Stinkingwater Mountains.

The second possible gold location, Hampton Butte and the Maury Mountains, seems a more likely site. The Cascade Range and Pilot Butte are clearly visible from Alkali Butte at the west end of the Maury Mountain range. Was the Cascade Range also visible from the west side of Hampton Butte? After considerable discussion, Clark and Tiller conclude that the discovery was probably made

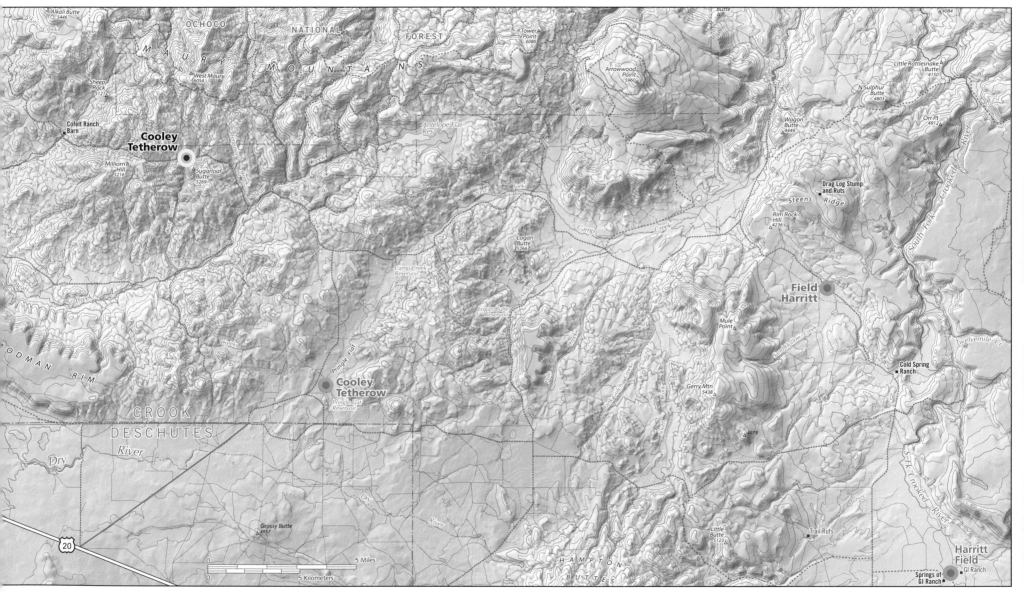

MAP 6 The Hampton Buttes—Maury Mountains

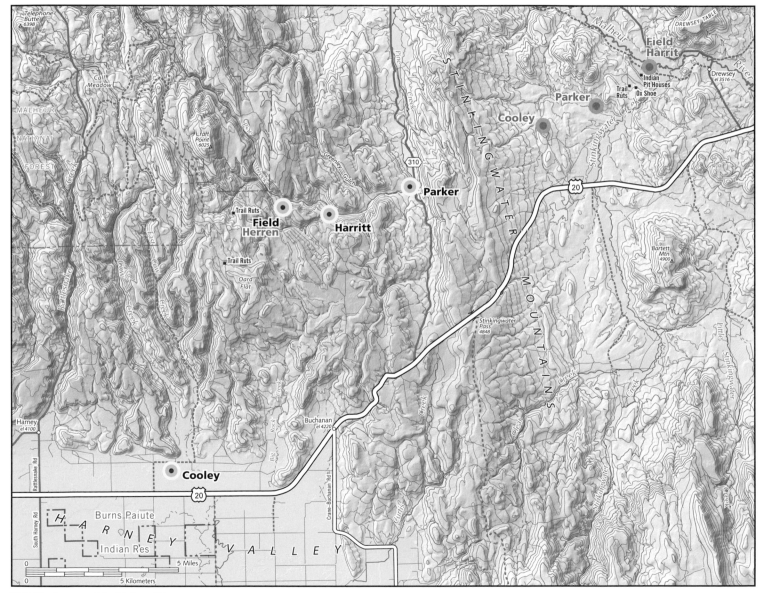

MAP 7 Headwaters of the Malheur River

by the Tetherow party at a location between Wagontire Mountain and Hampton Butte.

How should our expedition deal with this issue? It seemed to us that the most intelligent approach would be to establish the emigrants' route of travel, try to locate the appropriate campsites, and then ask an experienced gold prospector with a metal detector to search the most likely areas. We were aware that subsequent slides and geologic or man-made disturbances may have covered or destroyed the location of the purported gold site.

The expedition discovered a place that matches the geographical features of the gold discovery described by W. H. Herren. While we did not find the gold, the search added to the enjoyment of this whole experience. In any case, searching for lost gold sites, although good fun, is a highly speculative enterprise. Maybe the "discovery" is best left unresolved.

Stories of Blue Bucket gold have circulated throughout Oregon from 1845 until today. Prospectors and others searching for the legendary gold did make significant gold discoveries in the Powder River Basin, Baker River, and Canyon Creek Valley areas of eastern Oregon. These discoveries and the stories of the prospector's adventures in that part of the world encouraged settlement of the region.

THE JOURNEY, DAY TO DAY

NOTE TO THE READER

IN THE "DAY TO DAY" SECTION THAT FOLLOWS, each day's entry begins with a map and a summary of where each diarist traveled. The diaries themselves are presented in full at the end of the description of that day's travel. Through September 8, John Herren's diary entry is given first, because the company of which he was a member led the various wagon companies. As it was not possible to read his diary after September 8, we were left with only four diarists. Eli Cooley's diary is the only written record of the group that traveled along the south side of the Maury Mountains, reaching Cline Falls on the Deschutes River on September 25.

The reader will quickly realize that the diarists tended to spell phonetically. The words, even when misspelled, are easily understood, and we had to insert only a few bracketed explanations. A few recurring words that should be explained: as far as I can determine, "Cedar" refers to juniper trees; "drean" refers to a channel with or without water; "wormwood" is sagebrush.

SATURDAY, AUGUST 23, 1845

Herren, Cooley, and Parker traveled about fifteen miles to the present-day site of Vale on the Oregon Trail. Field and Harritt departed Fort Boise, crossed the Snake River, and camped on its west bank.

- - - - - - - - - - - - - - - - - - - - -

FROM FORT BOISE ON THE SNAKE RIVER, PART OF the emigrant group (Herren, Parker, and Cooley) traveled about fifteen miles over a gentle pass to the Malheur River and camped at what is now Vale, Oregon. Field and Harritt traveled to Fort Boise. They then crossed the Snake River and camped on the west bank, across from the fort. Arriving at this spot on September 2, 1845, Joel Palmer, one of the captains of the 1845 emigration and later author of an early published guide to the Oregon Trail, wrote, "At this place the road crosses the river, the ford is about 400 yards below the Fort, and strikes across to the head of an island, then bears to the left to the southern bank, the water is quite deep, but not rapid." Although the Snake River is now extensively dammed, a representative of the Idaho Power Company confirmed that the Snake River at the Fort Boise site still flows freely. To reach the site of the fort from Ontario, Oregon, take Highway 20–26 east into Idaho and then take the Fruitland Payette turnoff to Parma, Idaho. Go about ten miles and take a right turn onto the Old Fort Boise Road. Go west about four miles to the monument situated on the edge of the Snake River.

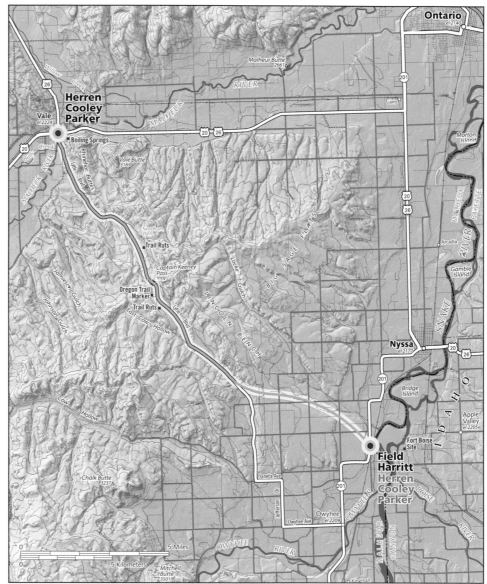

MAP 8 August 23, 1845

Paul Cronin standing next to the monument marking the site of Fort Boise. The Snake River can be seen through the trees on the right.

Oregon Trail marker at Keeney Pass.

The Snake River ford about four hundred yards south of Fort Boise, as seen from the Oregon side of the river. Photo by Richard Adams of Adams Art, Nyssa, OR.

Diarist James Field describes the fort as "a small, mean-looking fort, built like the others of sun-dried mud moulded into the shape of bricks, and appears more calculated for the collection of furs from other forts than for trading in its own immediate vicinity, as there is no game there."

Samuel Hancock, whose reminiscence is an important source of information on the Meek Cutoff, first met Steven Meek while camped at Fort Boise:

We encamped and remained a day. During this time a man whose name was Steven S. Meeks, (Meek) came along with a company of Parkers (packers) for Oregon; he said he had traveled the country between this point and Oregon many times and was quite familiar with the route; and that he would pilot us a near way that would save us a number of days' travel, provided that we would pay him for this service five dollars for each wagon in our train. We consulted with the Manager at Fort Boise, in

relation to this and he informed us that Mr. Meeks had passed the Fort three times to his knowledge, and also that he knew that there was a pack trail, through the country that Mr. Meeks designed going, so the most of us decided to follow him.

Although Joel Palmer was not present for the discussion on August 22 and 23, he effectively describes the fateful meeting between Meek and the emigrants as he heard about it a few days later:

Steve Lent on wagon ruts just east of the Keeney Pass overlook.

The Oregon Trail Mushroom Company and the hot springs at Vale, Oregon.

Hot Springs.

At this place are two trails; the fork is in the bottom above the crossing of the creek, and there is a possibility of emigrants pursuing the wrong route. I do not deem it amiss to give some particulars in relation to this road. Mr. Meek, who had been engaged as our pilot, but had previously went in advance of the companies who had employed him, and who had after reaching Fort Hall, fitted up a party to pilot through to Oregon, informed the emigrants that he could, by taking up this stream to near its source, and then striking across the plains, so as to intersect the old road near to the mouth of Deshutes or Falls river, save about one hundred and fifty miles travel; also that he was perfectly familiar with the country through which the proposed route lay, as he had traveled it; that no difficulty or danger attended its travel. He succeeded in inducing about two hundred families to pursue this route; they accordingly directed their course to the left, up this creek, about ten days previous to our arrival at the forks.

The Oregon Trail crosses Keeney Pass eight or nine miles northwest of Fort Boise on its way to Vale, Oregon. The pass, a gentle route through sagebrush, is identified as the "Oregon Trail Historic District" and administered by the BLM on what is now Lytle Boulevard. The trail is named for Jonathan Keeney, a mountain man who traversed large sections of the American West from 1831 to 1846 trapping and trading with the American Fur Company. He brought his family to Oregon with the 1846 migration and, after a variety of jobs including gold prospecting, he built and maintained a ferry on the Snake River near Fort Boise.

The overlook at Keeney Pass, the site of well-defined Oregon Trail wagon ruts, is about a third of a mile from the parking lot. We believe other ruts are still visible east of the overlook. Native grasses can still be seen along the path. It is a dramatic site.

Many Oregon Trail diaries mention the hot springs located at the east end of Vale, just west of the now bankrupt Oregon Trail Mushroom Company. Our photographs clearly show the steaming springs today, just as they appeared to the overlanders of 1845. Emigrants used the springs to bathe and wash their dirty clothes. Stories of the trail suggest that some emigrants were badly burned or killed by collapsing ground around the springs. From our walk around the springs, incidents of this kind seemed likely.

JOHN HERREN: *This morning our company was called together, for the purpose of hiring a pilot to conduct us across the bend in Boise River and over the Blue Mountains, down to the Dalles, on the Columbia River. This route will cut off the bend of the road that leads down Burnt River, and is said to be one hundred and fifty (150) miles nearer than the old route. Price agreed on with Mr. Meek to take us through the new route was fifty dollars. So we got up our oxen and started about 9 o'clock, and traveled a northwest course to a beautiful stream of water called Malheur, about twelve miles from where*

The Malheur River at Vale, August 2006.

we crossed the river, found plenty of grass and small willows to build a fire to get supper with, so there was no grumbling.

SAMUEL PARKER: *went to malhure Creek 16 [miles]*

ELI COOLEY: *Traveled to day. The road has been verry good. Weather fine. Come up a small valley and down an other to Mallaer River and camped. Plenty of grass and willow here. The corse has been to day a little North of West. They was an other company got to the crossing of the river to day.   10 miles*

JAMES FIELD: *Went four miles this morning, which took us to Fort Boise, which stands on the eastern bank of the Snake River near the mouth of the Boise. It is a small, mean-looking fort, built like the others of sun dried mud moulded into the shape of bricks, and appears more calculated for the collection of furs from other forts than for trading in its own immediate vicinity, as there is no game there, and the Indians living in this part of the country are very poor, many of them nearly naked and*

living on fish and roots. It was necessary to re-cross Snake River at this place, which is here fordable, and we all got safely over during the afternoon, camping on the western bank. The Indians assisted us in crossing, showing us the ford and helping us to drive the loose cattle, in return for which a few presents pleased them greatly. The river is near half a mile wide and so deep as to run over the tops of the wagon sides in places, but as it was generally of uniform depth all the way across, the current was not so rapid as at the other crossing.

JESSE HARRITT: *Four miles brought us down to Fort Boise. This fort is situated on the north bank of Lewis or Snake River and is owned by the Hudson's Bay Co.; crossed over to the south side where we encamped; found grass and a few small willows; the river here is about three-fourths of a mile wide; the water is about four feet deep and runs with a gentle current.*

SUNDAY, AUGUST 24

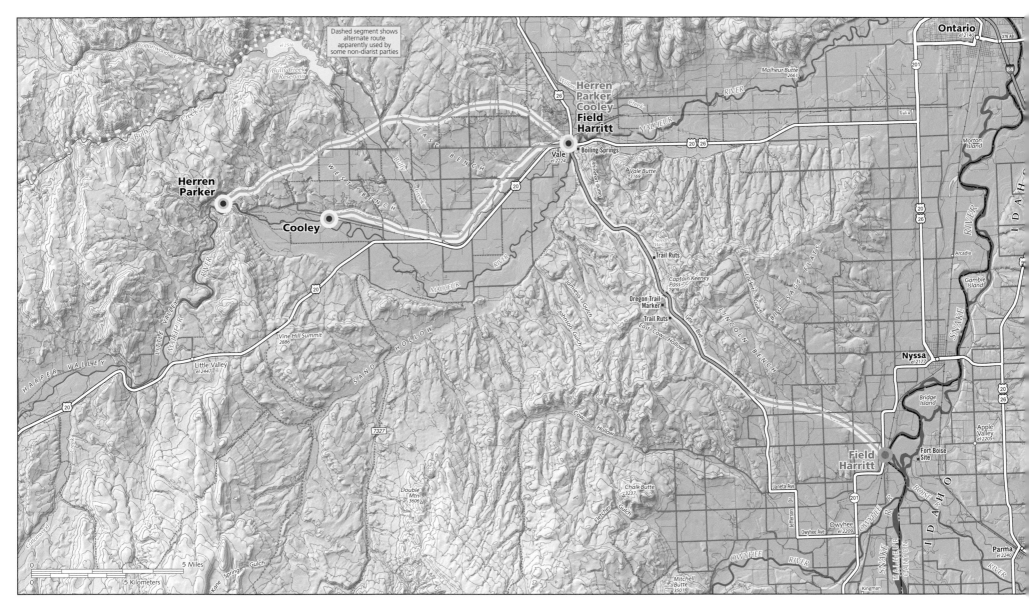

MAP 9 August 24, 1845

Herren and Parker traveled twelve to fourteen miles and camped on the north side of the Malheur River west of Vale. Cooley apparently traveled eight miles and camped on the north side of the Malheur River. Field and Harritt traveled twelve to sixteen miles to Herren's Vale campsite.

The Malheur River west of Vale, Oregon.

FIELD'S DETAILED DIARY COMMENTS ARE WORTH noting, as he worries about Indians and explains why his company decided to follow Meek.

Today, much of the ground five to ten miles west of Vale is farmland under active cultivation and irrigation. Crops include a wide variety of vegetables such as onions, potatoes, and sugar beets, as well as alfalfa. Our expedition was unlikely to find ruts or artifacts in such an area. After consulting topographic maps and viewing the landscape from a hill above the north side of the river, we found our way to a beautiful spot along the Malheur River, which at this point is a free-flowing low-bank stream ten to thirty feet wide.

We could see why the emigrants had been attracted to this site, which Herren describes as a place with plenty of water, grass, and dry willows for a fire. The area near the river had many trees and ample grass. As we moved away from the river, sagebrush and dust became more prevalent. Herren mentions the dust in his diary entry for the twenty-fourth and Field, traveling the same route a day later, writes:

> Since crossing to this side of the Snake River again the road has been fearfully dusty. In fact, a person who has never traveled these wormwood barrens can form no idea as to what depth dust may be cut up in them by the passing of a few wagons. To a person walking in the road it is frequently more than shoe deep, and if the wind happens to blow lengthwise of the road, it raises such a fog that you cannot see the next wagon in front.

Expedition member Bob Boyd told us that the wagons, if observed from the air, would have resembled a series of moving dust clouds. Since the two hundred wagons had separated months before into smaller groups with their own stock of animals, each grouping created its own dust storm. Not incidentally, hygiene issues also encouraged the emigrants to travel in smaller groups. Twelve hundred emigrants would average six to a wagon. Imagine the sanitary requirements for one company of perhaps twenty wagons, 120 people, camping in the sagebrush or along a stream or creek. Dust and hygiene along with issues of leadership were the main reasons wagon trains separated into smaller companies.

Field's usage of the term "roads" refers to the route traveled by the emigrants and to the ruts of the Oregon Trail. There was no "road" or trail as we understand those words although there may have been a faint pack trail up part of the Malheur. The diarists often use the word "road," but it refers to the trail they were creating. Cattle, horses, and other livestock often wandered away from the encampments searching for water or food. Indians occasionally stole livestock. Herren notes an occurrence on this day.

HERREN: *More oxen missing this morning. 11 o'clock before all the wagons were out of camp, traveled about*

The Malheur River plain looking east toward Vale. We found probable campsites along the river.　Searching for artifacts.

12 miles, 6 first miles northwest, then changed our course to southwest until we came to same stream of water that we encamped on last night, and found plenty of water and grass and dry willows to make fire with. The route to-day has been dry and uncommonly dusty, and entirely destitute of timber or vegetation of any kind, except wild sage, and it is dying very fast for want of rain; country tolerably level but not fit for cultivation. The Indians stole one horse last night within thirty yards of our encampment.

PARKER: *tuck what is caled the meeks Cut of   Missas But tuck [Mrs. Butts took] Sick this day　A Bad Cut of fore all that tuck it*

COOLEY: *Mr. Meek this morning started to pilot us the new rout. Wee left the old rout and turned to the left. Crossed the Mallaer River whare wee camped and have traveled up it to day though only in site of it until wee camped. Struck it and camped on it. The road has been verry good. Weather fine. The corse has been nearly west.　8 miles*

FIELD: *The story of the murder of the two Frenchmen by the Walla Wallas is pronounced a humbug by the people of the fort. They say that the Walla Wallas entertain a hostile feeling toward us, and will probably try to injure us as we pass through their territory, but their numbers or their equipment would not render them dangerous to such sized companies as we are in at present. Still, the nature of the country is such that if they took advantage of it they could damage us considerably. We have traveled thus far as three companies without any general commander, and previous to our starting this morning it was agreed to choose one. Accordingly, James B. Riggs, our own old captain, was elected captain of the whole company by a unanimous vote. A man named Meek has engaged to pilot the leading company, Capt. Owensby's, which is the only one now ahead of us. He was to guide the outfit through to the Dalles of the Columbia River by a new and nearer route, following the pack trail from Fort Boise and missing the Walla Wallas altogether, leaving Fort Walla Walla on his right and cutting off between 100 and 200 miles travel. A vote was taken wheather we should follow them or keep the old way, and a majority decided on the new one. We traveled about 16 miles, camping upon Malheur Creek near the forks of two roads.*

HARRITT: *Leaving the river we traveled in a southwest course over a good road; made an advance of twelve miles and encamped on a stream affording grass and willows.*

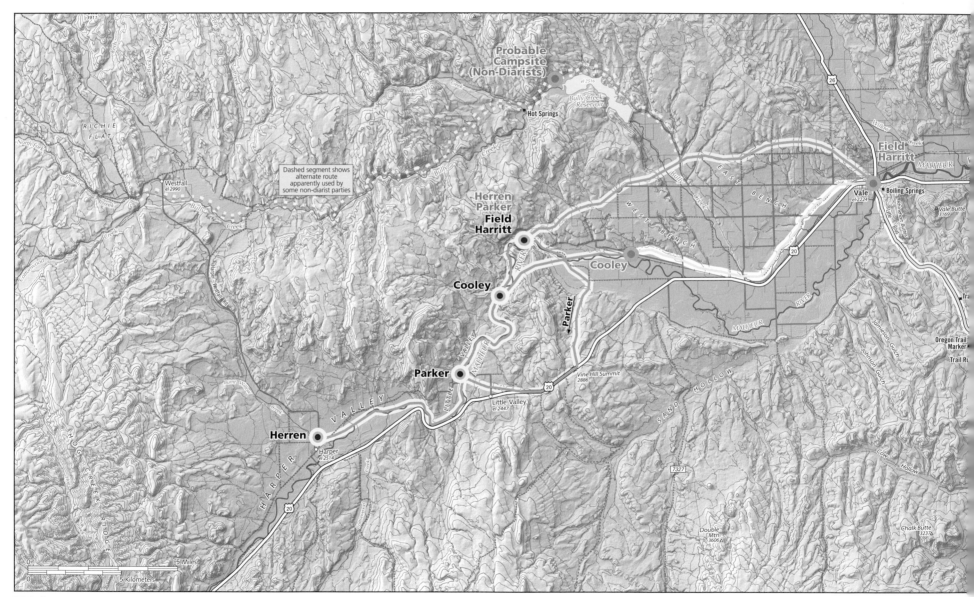

MAP 10 August 25, 1845

Herren traveled ten miles, probably along the north side of the Malheur River, to a site near Harper. Parker traveled fourteen miles, probably over Vines Hill on the south side of the Malheur River, and camped a few miles from Herren. Cooley moved only six miles, crossed and re-crossed the Malheur River, and camped somewhere west of Field and Harritt. Harritt and Field traveled thirteen and eleven miles, respectively, and camped near Herren's August 24 site.

- -

HERREN TRAVELED TEN MILES WEST ALONG THE Malheur River. The expedition's calculations agree with Del Hinshaw's suggested campsite locations. Herren probably camped near the present-day site of Harper. Parker appears to have taken a different route, probably over Vines Hill, south of the Malheur gorge and now the route of Highway 20 from Vale to Harper. It is a dry, sagebrush-covered rise, but it would have offered the emigrants spectacular views (although I suspect views were of little interest to the emigrants). The alternate line of travel along the Malheur River was a shorter but more difficult trail. Parker descended the hill late in the day and camped on the Malheur River, probably near Herren's camp. Cooley moved only six miles and camped for the night near Harritt and Field,

who were a day behind. They probably camped where the Herren and Parker groups had camped the previous evening.

From the campsite on August 24, the Herren wagons followed the twists and turns of the Malheur River, which flows through some five miles of rugged, winding gorges. Field, on August 26, one day behind Herren, writes: "Still keeping up Malheur, crossing and re-crossing it twice, and camping upon it. We were obliged to take to the bluffs to get across several narrow bends of the river, and we there found some as hard road as any we had yet traveled. Indeed, I begin to think wagons can go anywhere." This is rocky, inhospitable country. The Malheur gorge then opens into a flat area that in 1845 was probably covered with sagebrush but today consists of beautiful cultivated fields, known as Little Valley. Cultivation has destroyed any trace of campsites or ruts in this area.

Written reminiscences, coupled with comments from older residents living in the area, some of whom are descendants of pioneer families, strongly suggest that some parts of the non-diarist Meek party traveled up Bully Creek and camped near hot springs above the Bully Creek Reservoir.

In the opinion of our expedition members, however, all of the diarists went upstream on the Malheur River or over Vines Hill. The companies had outriders who rode ahead to determine the best route for the wagons. The outriders may or may not have met up with the slower-traveling parties, but

The Malheur River gorge before the river settles into Little Valley. Vines Hill is on the left.

Little Valley. "There are some willows and grass is very good on the low bottoms near the creek" (Herren diary).

one way or another word of the rough trail along the river must have filtered back to the groups behind, and those emigrants chose an arguably less arduous route up Bully Creek.

Some of the expedition members drove to Bully Creek Reservoir, a 985-acre lake. The reservoir was built by the Bureau of Reclamation in 1963 and has seven miles of shoreline. We met Bob Jordan there. He is associated with the management of the reservoir and is thoroughly familiar with local stories about the members of the Meek party who reputedly took the Bully Creek route. Standing on the road well west of the west end of the reservoir, Jordan pointed toward a heavily treed area where local residents believe some of the parties camped. There, Bully Creek runs through a large grove of cottonwood, Russian olive, and willows, and then becomes the west shore of the reservoir. I imagine the grove looks today about as it did in 1845. Approximately half a mile west of the campground, hot sulfur springs flow out of the hill on the north side of the road. The odor of sulfur is very noticeable.

Another two or three hundred yards west of the springs, Bob Jordan pointed to a draw on the left. Bob and others believe the emigrants exited through the draw on their way to a camp near what is now the town of Westfall.

HERREN: *Started about 8 o'clock and encamped about 4. Traveled over some very rough road to-day, the fords of the creek very rough and rocky, the country very poor and*

The campground west of Bully Creek Reservoir.

The hot springs a half mile west of the campground at Bully Creek Reservoir.

broken, no timber only along the water courses. There are some willows and grass is very good on the low bottoms near the creek. Course to-day generally southwest, distance about ten miles.

PARKER: *went over hills all day and Came to the malhuren at nite 14*

COOLEY: *Traveled up Mallear to day. Come about 1 mile and 1/2 and crossed the River and in a few hundred yards crossed it again and in about 1 mile crossed again and in a short distance crossed again and thare turned to the rite up the bluff and in about 2 miles struck it again. Went 1/2 mile up it and camped. Plenty of grass and willow here. The road to whare wee crossed the first time is verry good; it then is quite broken and rough to whare wee struck it the last time; it then is verry good. Weather fine to day.   6 miles*

FIELD: *Went about 11 miles across the hills, camping on Malheur River again. Since crossing to this side of the Snake River again the road has been fearfully dusty. In fact, a person who has never traveled these wormwood barrens can form no idea as to what depth dust may be cut up in them by the passing of a few wagons. To a person walking in the road it is frequently more than shoe deep, and if the wind happens to blow lengthwise of the road, it raises such a fog that you cannot see the next wagon in front.*

HARRIT: *Here we left the former route, bearing a little south of west; we steered our course over a tolerable good road thirteen miles and encamped on the same stream, found grass and fine willows.*

The saddle the emigrants traveled as they left Bully Creek.

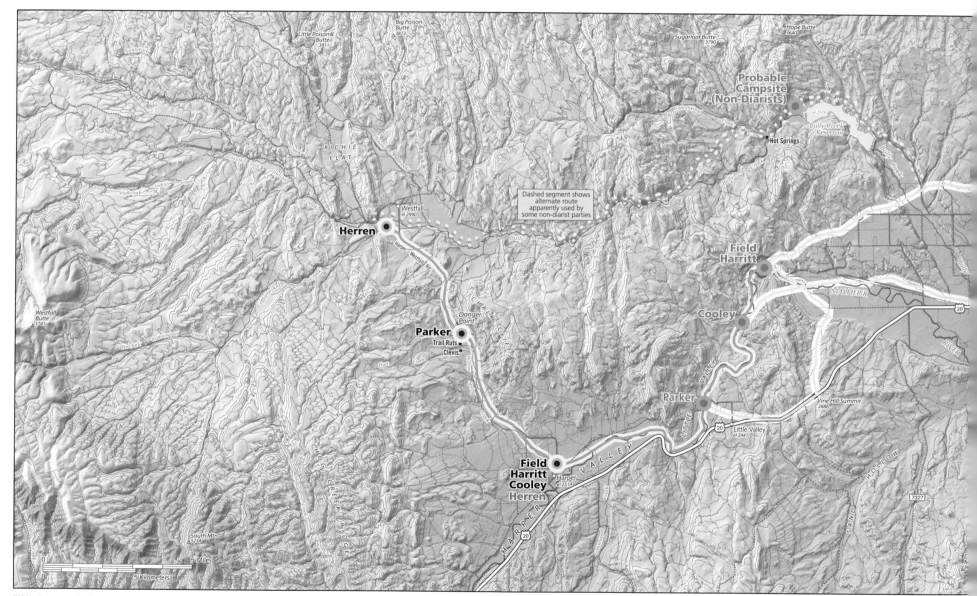

MAP 11 August 26, 1845

Herren traveled eighteen miles up Spring Creek to and probably beyond the present tiny community of Westfall. Parker traveled fourteen miles and may have camped south of Westfall.

Cooley, Harritt, and Field, from their diary descriptions, traveled twelve, ten, and ten miles, respectively, and probably camped near Harper. All three seemed to travel over and around the rocky bluffs along the Malheur River between their August 25 campsite and Harper.

HERREN TRAVELED EIGHTEEN MILES NORTHWEST of the Harper campsite. We believe he reached an area, now cultivated, one to two miles northwest of Westfall. This would place Herren at the campsite identified by Del Hinshaw. While much of the surrounding area is sagebrush, the suggested site has some trees and other vegetation. This location is only an educated guess. The expedition searched carefully for the "boiling spring" referred to in Herren's diary entry but did not find it. We spoke with ranchers in the area but they were unaware of any such springs. Springs that were present in 1845 may have dried out or gone underground in the intervening 161 years from 1845 to 2006.

The chalk bluffs at Danger Point.

Examining trail ruts.

The pillar at Danger Point.

Waiting to see what the metal detector located.

The clevis in its bed.

A clevis exhumed.

Incidentally, the term "balm" Herren mentions refers to resins from tropical trees or plants of the mint family. Herren may simply be describing the low-lying vegetation that covers some of the desert floor, particularly near watered areas.

As we drove from Harper to Westfall along the edge of a broad sagebrush valley, expedition member Bob Boyd pointed out ruts he had found years ago just west of Danger Point on the Harper-Westfall road. We first searched a rock pillar, some fifty feet high and located adjacent to the road, for any inscriptions, since the emigrants were occasionally known to leave marks, but we found nothing. Then expedition members spread out and walked west through the sagebrush.

We located and photographed the ruts. Those with metal detectors then went to work. Walking slowly, the operators held rods with a flat coil just inches above the ground. An electronic device located on the rod produced signals, a series of beeps that grew in intensity as the detector closed in on the target. Within half an hour, Margi Heater found a clevis, a U-shaped metal fastener used in a wagon-train undercarriage, under fifteen inches of topsoil. We were confident we were walking in the ruts of the 1845 trail. After photographing the clevis, we placed it back in its hole, carefully following BLM rules, and Art McEldowney noted its GPS location.

Harritt and Parker traveled a few miles behind Herren. Both journeyed between ten and fourteen miles and probably camped separately southeast of Westfall, perhaps near the site of our discovery. Field, a day behind, traveled along the Malheur River, probably camping near Herren's Harper campsite. From Cooley's diary description, he may have camped near Field.

HERREN: *Started about half past seven. Still keeping up Malheur creek and crossed it the second time, then we left it and turned into a gap into the Blue Mountains, over some tolerably rough road near our encampment and on the east of it was a boiling spring that afforded water enough where we found first-rate water and grass and willows, and a kind of soft wood called Balm. Distance, eighteen miles.*

PARKER: *Verry Rockey and hilly Camped on A small streame 14*

COOLEY: *Left the River this morning and in about 1 mile struck it again and crossed 2 and come up about 2 miles and left it and come about 9 mile and camped on a drean. Plenty of grass, wood and water. Road quite rough. Weather fine. 12 miles*

FIELD: *Went about ten miles, still keeping up Malheur, crossing and re-crossing it twice, and camping upon it. We were obliged to take to the bluffs to get across several narrow bends of the river, and we there found some as hard road as any we had yet traveled. Indeed, I begin to think wagons can go anywhere.*

HARRITT: *Proceeded ten miles further up the creek and encamped; found grass and fine willows; had about four miles of very bad road; balance good.*

The ruts as they appear from the air. Note the pillar in the right upper background.

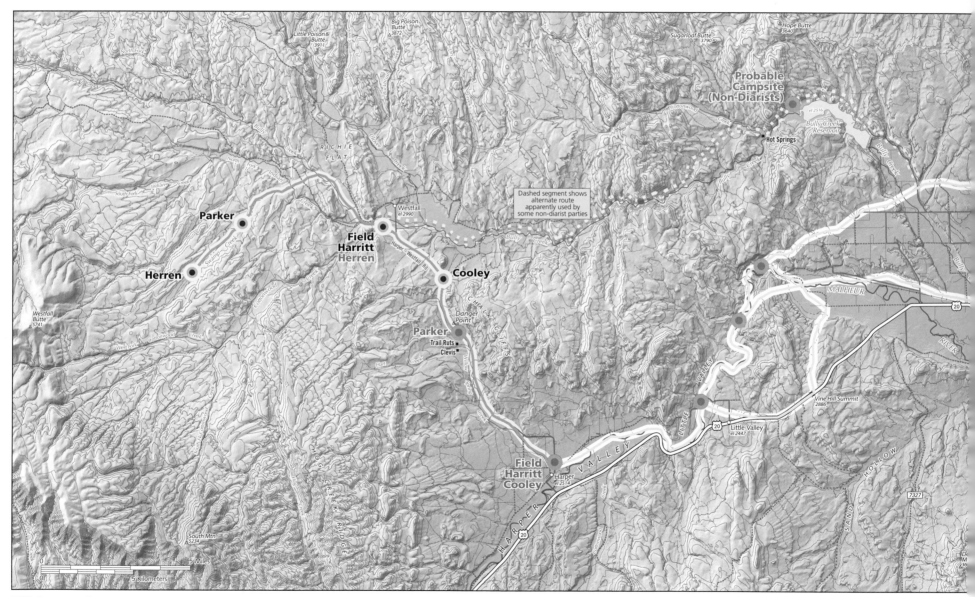

Probable
Campsite
(Non-Diarists)

el 2516

Bully Creek
Reservoir

Hot Springs

Dashed segment shows
alternate route
apparently used by
some non-diarist parties

Westfall
el 2990

Parker

Field
Harritt
Herren

Herren

Cooley

Bully Creek

Westfall
Butte
5741

Danger
Point

CHALK CLIFFS

MALHEUR

20

Parker

Trail Ruts
Clevis

Vine Hill Summit
2886

Little Valley

20

Little Valley
el 2447

Field
Harritt
Cooley

Harper
el 2514

HARPER VALLEY

SAND HOLLOW

7327

South Mtn
5234

HOG CREEK RIDGE

20

0   5 Miles

0   5 Kilometers

MAP 12 August 27, 1845

Paul Cronin coming up the trail. To the east, between and below the buttes, is the tiny town of Westfall.

Herren traveled ten miles and camped on or near Swamp Creek. Parker traveled twelve miles and camped a few miles short of Swamp Creek. Field traveled eighteen miles and probably camped at Herren's August 26 site, northwest of Westfall. Harritt traveled twelve miles and probably camped in Herren's August 26 campsite. (Harritt's odometer may have been malfunctioning, since Harritt and Field tended to camp together.) Cooley moved just five miles, perhaps south of Danger Point.

- -

HERREN, LEADING THE WAY, TRAVELED TEN MILES and probably camped on or near Swamp Creek. Readers should remember that Herren was traveling with the Nicholas Ownbey company (see p. 15), as were Meek, W. A. Goulder, and Samuel Hancock, whose reminiscences offer significant insight into the route of travel. Harritt and Parker, apparently traveling near each other, appear to have camped west of Herren's August 26 campsite. Field moved eighteen miles and probably camped near Harritt and Parker. Cooley, trailing nearly a day behind, camped near Danger Point. The other diarists probably were strung out behind Ownbey. Apparently, some of the nondiarist groups were as much as five days behind Ownbey. While outriders mentioned some commu-

The white carsonite trail marker; we are looking east toward Westfall.

nication between the companies, it seems that each group was very much on its own.

Our expedition drove on a good dirt road traveling west of Westfall, eleven miles northwest of Harper. After traveling three or four miles from Westfall, Bob Boyd and Steve Lent, experienced trail-finders, suggested we park and walk through the sagebrush. After a few hundred yards, we discovered faint ruts winding through the sagebrush.

Then, to our surprise, we found a white post that read "Oregon Historic Trail." According to Randall Brown, a representative of the Oregon California Trail Association, the association placed the post, a carsonite (a fiberglass stake with a marker), to identify the trail. The only marker we discovered during the entire five weeks of our journey, it sits in the middle of barely discernible ruts heading west. Only an occasional juniper marred an unbroken

vista across sagebrush-covered flats. It was a hot, dusty, and desolate location.

Returning to our vehicles, we followed dirt roads, occasionally stopping to examine faint rut traces. We did find a possible trail two or three miles farther west of the marker.

A mile or two later, Bob Boyd and Art McEldowney located the site of Herren's August 27 camp. The site corresponded to the location Del Hinshaw listed in his annotated notebook, a copy now in the author's possession: "All gone today—replaced by a big ranch. The spring irrigates a vast alfalfa field. August 19, 1973—I was there. *DH*"

Herren's diary describes a cover of willows and some grass, but the character of the land and the terrain has changed dramatically over the intervening 168 years. Today the place is simply an inhospitable cattle-watering hole. The trees have disappeared. The stream is dry and only a little green grass remains. For any readers who want to retrace the search, be warned that part of the road to the August 27 campsite is deeply rutted and almost impassable.

Field, traveling a day behind Herren, notes that their party had begun to see "an abundance of small, sharp stones . . . black and hard as iron, and very wearing on the feet of the cattle." The landscape became more inhospitable as we drove west. Ahead of us, we saw miles of small sharp basalt stones running up to the base of Westfall Butte. Photos from

the August 28 day of travel will give the reader some idea of the emigrants' growing problem.

Describing the same area, Hancock wrote in his reminiscences, "We arrived at an exceedingly rough mountainous place, where we had to establish our road as we went, over a country never traveled perhaps by human being, save the trapper in pursuit of game, or roving savages."

HERREN: *Late start this morning; nine oxen missing. 11 o'clock before all of the wagons were out of camp, then we moved off a southwest course about ten miles to the head of the same branch that we camped on last night; had some very rough road to-day, passed down one very rocky ravine the valley of the little stream where we are to-night, and had it very dusty down the branch, found plenty of water and some willows, grass not good, very much dried up, mountains entirely barren, no soil here.*

PARKER: *Bad Road went 12*

COOLEY: *The road quite broken and rough to day. Weather fine. Left the hollow and in about 2 mile struck it again and traveled up it about 3 mile and camped. Some wood, grass and water here. 5 miles*

FIELD: *Went about 18 miles today. The road, although leading across the bluffs which in a country in which mountains are a rarity would pass for pretty good sized ones, was tolerably fair, but there is an abundance of small, sharp stones in it, black and hard as iron, and*

The carsonite trail marker from the air. Note the wagon ruts, to the right, and west from the marker. A good dirt road runs to the right of the 1845 trail.

The trail west of the carsonite marker.

Herren's probable campsite.

Lunch on the trail.

These may be trail ruts.

An aerial view of the campsite.

Millions of tiny stones; Westfall Butte in the background.

very wearing on the feet of the cattle. We camped upon Carter's fork, from its appearance a branch of Burnt River.

HARRITT: *Commenced winding our way through the Blue Mountains; at noon we left the pleasant stream to the left, turning gradually to the northwest; traveled over a tolerable bad road; reached the head of a small sinking rivulet affording excellent water and timber, cottonwood, willow and alder, the latter being the principal part, of which there is some of the largest I ever saw, measuring from twelve to fourteen inches in diameter; traveled twelve miles.*

THURSDAY, AUGUST 28

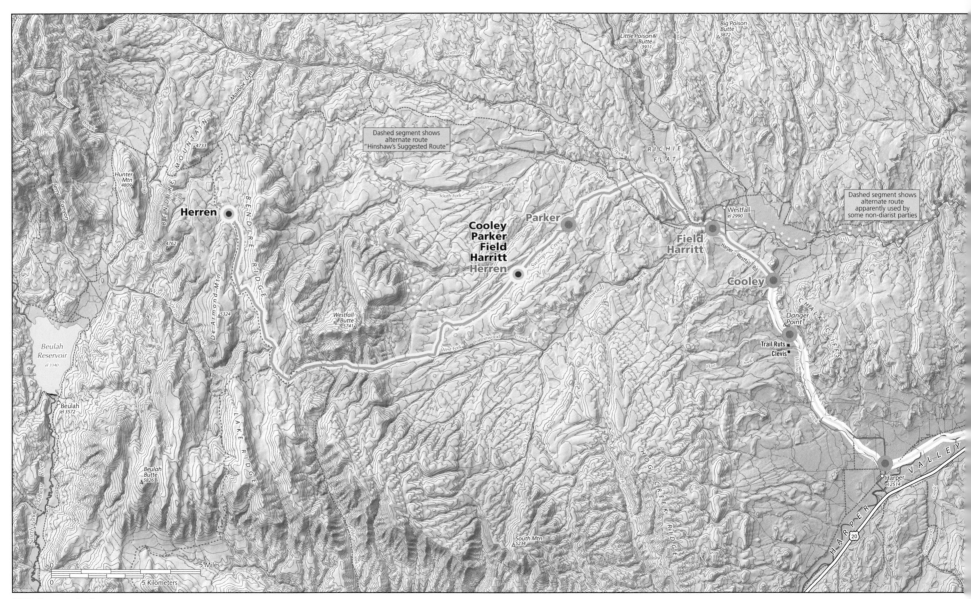

Dashed segment shows alternate route "Hinshaw's Suggested Route"

Dashed segment shows alternate route apparently used by some non-diarist parties

Herren

Cooley
Parker
Field
Harritt
Herren

Parker

Field
Harritt

Westfall
el 2990

Cooley

Danger Point

Trail Ruts
Clevis

Beulah Reservoir
el 3340

Beulah
Butte
3572

Beulah
el 3572

Westfall
Butte
5741

Hunter
Mtn
4809

South Mtn
5234

Harper
el 2514

MAP 13 August 28, 1845

52

Ruts adjacent to Pole Creek Road with Castle Rock in the background.

Looking into the gorge south of Westfall Butte. Steep hillsides converge on a narrow, rocky bottom.

Herren traveled eighteen rocky miles, possibly southwest around the base of Westfall Butte, and camped west of Bendire Ridge. Parker traveled seven miles, keeping a few miles ahead of Harritt, possibly camping south of Westfall Butte. Harritt traveled only five miles and must have camped on or near Swamp Creek. Field traveled six miles, probably to Swamp Creek. Cooley, moving twelve miles, may have caught up with Field.

- -

HERREN, UNDER PRESSURE TO REACH GRASS AND water, traveled some eighteen miles. The course of travel over the stone field took a terrible toll on the emigrants and their animals. In his diary, he writes that he traveled on a southwest course, but his route is uncertain. Some believe he traveled to Buckaroo or Butterfly Springs, south of Westfall Butte. The expedition visited both sites and found the route to these two locations extremely difficult to reach and well off the most economical line of travel. Going to either of the springs would require traversing very steep and rocky slopes.

Another possible route would have been south around the base of Westfall Butte, the route suggested by Del Hinshaw. It was a more direct traverse than climbing the slopes south of Westfall Butte to the two springs. Herren refers to a mountain about "three miles high" and Westfall Butte, at its base, looked very high indeed. But, when we investigated the land around the south base of Westfall Butte, we found a virtually impassable gorge.

We drove up to the flat area above the gorge. While the "flats" would have made for easy traveling, we could not find a convenient access to them. And there remains Herren's comment about passing a mountain "about three miles high." While Westfall Butte's elevation is only 5,744 feet, the imposing sight might have suggested a much higher number to the anxious emigrants if, indeed, they did somehow travel around the south side of the mountain.

We found well-defined ruts part way up the slope to the south and west of the butte that might have been the ruts from the 1845 train. The ruts are just west of Pole Creek Road coming up the grade from the south side of Westfall Butte. Castle Rock, then known as Fremont's Peak, clearly comes into view as the ruts are followed northwest up to a saddle. Castle Rock is mentioned in Field's diary of August 31, so the emigrants obviously recognized

The "flats" south of Westfall Butte. Between the butte and the terrace is a steep and narrow gorge.

Looking east toward Westfall Butte. A possible line of travel might be along the hills on the far right.

Looking west toward Westfall Butte in the distance.

the peak. Castle Rock, with an elevation of 6,818 feet and distinctive in its formation, can be seen for many miles in every direction. It rises 1,600 feet above the surrounding area.

There is another saddle on the north side of Westfall Butte west of the Gregory Creek Reservoir. While no ruts were found, this possible route looks reasonably level. Either a south or north route could have led to Hinshaw's suggested campsite west of Bendire Ridge, or nondiarist companies may have used both.

Harritt also reports a southwest course of travel. Parker comments on the rough road, so it appears he was moving along the ridges south of Westfall Butte. He reports traveling seven miles. Field appears to have camped somewhere near Herren's August 27 campsite. Cooley's diary description suggests he is in rocky terrain with Field.

All of the diarists comment on the rough stony road. Oxen and horses were badly injured and some were simply abandoned. Field writes, "The sharp stones spoken of yesterday were more plentiful today, and a few more such days travel as this will entirely use up our cattle's feet." Herren notes that the oxen, cattle and horses suffered "over some of the worst road that they have traveled over yet, for it was uncommonly rocky and hilly." Expedition members noted that even our good hiking shoes would not last long in this terrain.

HERREN: *Made an early start this morning. Our pilot told us we had 18 miles to go to grass and water. So we traveled off at a quick pace but found no water, only a small spring that did not afford water enough to drink, so our poor oxen, cattle and horses had to suffer for water another night after a hard day's travel over some of the worst road that they have traveled over yet, for it was uncommonly rocky and hilly. We passed up one mountain to-day that was about three miles high besides several that were from 1/2 to 3/4 of a mile high, and down some that were very near a mile slope. Passed some cedar, though they were small; grass good; course today southwest.*

80 miles from Boise River.

The rocky plain east of Westfall Butte.

PARKER: *Bad Road went 7*

COOLEY: *The road to day has been verry broken and rough to day. Had some rain to nite. Traveled up the hollow over some verry large hills. About 9 mile is a small spring near the road and about 3 mile further some out of the way to the left whare wee camped is a small spring and some wood and grass. Some oxen give out today.   12 miles*

FIELD: Went *about 6 miles, camping upon the same branch as before. The sharp stones spoken of yesterday were more plentiful today, and a few more such days travel as this will entirely use up our cattle's feet.*

HARRITT: *Turned to the southwest; passed over a range of mountains; had bad roads; traveled five miles and encamped on a small stream; found but little grass— wood plenty.*

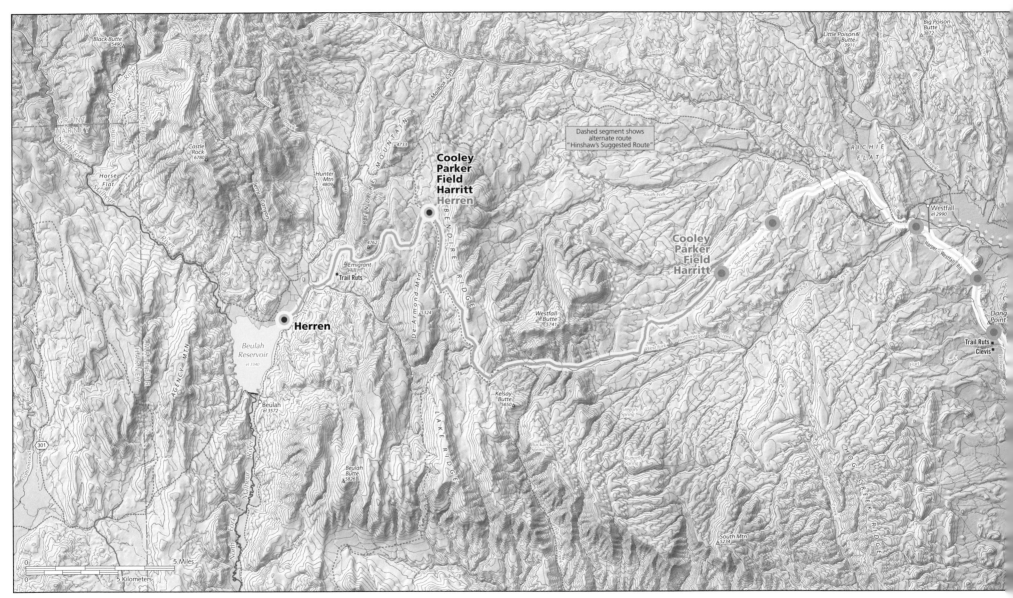

MAP 14 August 29, 1845

Herren traveled nine miles, to or near the hot spring at the northeast corner of Beulah Reservoir. Harritt traveled twelve miles from the Swamp Creek area probably to Herren's August 28 campsite. Parker went just five miles and camped near Harritt. Field and Cooley each traveled six miles and probably camped near Harritt and Parker.

HERREN TRAVELED NINE MILES AND PROBABLY camped on Warm Springs Creek near the northeast corner of what today is Beulah Reservoir. The Butler Beulah Ranch is headquartered a mile or so northeast of the reservoir. Emigrant Hill, also known as Immigrant Hill, was named by residents of the area. It is located in the northeast quadrant of the ranch. According to Bill Butler, the owner of the ranch, and his daughter Robin, the hill marks a place of a steep descent by the emigrants into the Warm Springs Creek watershed.

Reminiscences describe ruts and large gashes on the landscape where the wagons rolled and skidded out of the mountains and descended to Warm Springs Creek. Keith Clark and Lowell Tiller note that "the scars of their descent were still visible on the west side of Immigrant Hill in June, 1960." On the west shoulder of Emigrant Hill, we found ruts and substantial gashes in the sagebrush as well as

A trail trace coming off the lower reaches of Emigrant Hill.

ax-hewn juniper stumps covered in subsequent growth. We do not know if the U.S. Army or Miller and Lux, a previous landowner, or the U.S. Indian Service followed the Meek Trail and improved on it or to what extent the Meek Trail provided the basis for others traveling through the area.

All the expedition members climbed the lower stretches of the hill to photograph the ruts, but Steve Lent took a two-hour round trip walk in 98-degree heat straight up the hill looking for further evidence. On returning, his first words were, "That's one hell of a lot farther than it looks!"—a common lament of rut rats.

Harritt, traveling a day behind and apparently following in Herren's path, comments on the hot springs that cascade from the banks of Warm Springs Creek near the Herren campsite: "a warm spring bursting from the side of a lofty mountain, a little above blood heat." He says the spring provided sufficient water for human use, but was insufficient for the stock. We found the springs as Harritt described them.

Field likely traveled with Harritt a day behind

Steve Lent after returning from climbing Emigrant Hill in the background— 98 degrees!

Herren and camped near Parker, Cooley, and Harritt. He again comments on the stony road: "The mountains are covered with small, black, hard, nine-cornered stones, about the size of those used to macadamize a road, and our cattle cringe at every step." In an undated narrative, Samuel Hancock describes a similar terrain, cruel to animals:

Sometimes for the distance of many miles the entire surface of the Country was covered with a medium sized stone or boulder, just large enough to make it difficult to travel over them; the only way the teams behind could distinguish the route was by the bruised and broken boulders, occasioned by the wheels of the front wagons passing over them, and the blood from the feet of our poor animals that suffered almost beyond endurance, for in many instances they would lie down and suffer any kind of punishment in preference to rising, and frequently we were obliged to leave them lying upon the rocks where nothing could be obtained for them to eat.

Cooley's odometer mileage numbers do not match any of the other diary figures. He records only six miles, but his odometer may have been malfunctioning due to the rough terrain. His August 30 diary confirms that he reached the North Fork of the Malheur River at what is now Beulah Reservoir, and in all likelihood camped near Harritt, Parker, and Field.

Parker also comments on the bad road and writes that his company "broak 3 wagens this day." While Parker's odometer may have been inaccurate (his mileage at that point does not correspond to today's maps), he only records five miles, probably following Herren's trail.

In summary, Herren appears to be a day in the lead, with the remaining diarists traveling his path about a day behind.

The expedition, in an effort to follow Del Hinshaw's route around Westfall Butte, took an extremely rough road east from Beulah Reservoir to Bendire Ridge. It required an hour and a half to make approximately ten miles to the base of the ridge. The road was full of large jagged rocks and was the worst road we experienced on our journey.

Along the west base of Bendire Ridge, we found green grass but no flowing water. Metal detectors found nothing. Still, Hinshaw had told both the BLM archaeologists and Bob Boyd that some of the emigrants camped in this area prior to arriving at Warm Springs Creek at the north end of Beulah Reservoir. It required more imagination than we possessed to see any sign of tracks on Bendire Ridge or near the possible campsite.

HERREN: *This morning we left our dry encampment and traveled about 3/4 of a mile a northwest course, then turning a northeast course, one mile, then north 3/4 of a mile, then we turned northwest about 3 miles and passed up a mountain about one mile high; here we changed*

Warm Springs Creek where it enters the northeast section of Beulah Reservoir.

Hot springs near Herren's August 29 campsite on Warm Springs Creek. The water, indeed, is a little above "blood heat."

Possible camping spot west of Bendire Ridge.

our course to west about one mile to the top of another mountain, here we discovered water and grass sufficient about 3-1/2 miles off, so we turned a southwest course over some as rocky road as ever I want to travel, for our wagons were off one rock on to another all of the way down the slope of the mountain, which occasioned a mighty jolting and rumbling with old wagons, for both men and cattle were in a hurry to get to water. We found a beautiful little stream of excellent water and plenty of grass, and willows that were dry and some cedar to make a fire with. We passed considerable cedar timber, but it was low and scrubby. We had considerable rain this evening. Distance nine miles.

PARKER: *Verry bad Road   Broak 3 wagens this day   5*

COOLEY: *The road to day has been quite broken and rough. To day weather fine. Road quite crooked. Come about 6 miles and camped on a hill. Plenty of grass and willow here. West the general corse has been about.   6 miles.*

FIELD: *Went about 12 miles today, over mountains to which those we had previously crossed were small hills, camping near a little spring in the mountains which affords sufficient water for the use of the camp, but our cattle would have been obliged to do without any had it not been for a storm of rain which came on in the evening, the first storm for months. The mountains are covered with small, black, hard, nine-cornered stones, about the size of those used to macadamize a road, and our cattle cringe at every step.*

HARRITT: *Traveled 12 miles over the mountain; had bad road; encamped at a good spring, affording plenty of water for camp use; none for stock; found tolerable good grass and a few willows.*

SATURDAY, AUGUST 30

Herren traveled five miles and camped on the North Fork of the Malheur River some three or four miles northwest of Beulah Reservoir. Harritt moved ten miles and camped at Herren's August 29 site on the hot spring at the northeast corner of Beulah Reservoir. Parker made eleven miles, and Field made twelve. They both camped near Harritt. Cooley ventured only four miles according to his odometer, which may still have been malfunctioning. He reached the North Fork of the Malheur and therefore must have been with or near Field, Parker, and Harritt. Moreover, as the four diarists traveled only five miles on the thirty-first to a site described in similar terms by each of the four, it is likely they were traveling together.

- -

HERREN TRAVELED SEVERAL MILES UP THE NORTH Fork of the Malheur River. He notes, "Grass very good and plenty of Willows, Alder, and Balm on the mountains. Some cedar but they are small and low; the mountains where we are now are covered with grass."

The expedition members are certain that Herren's August 30 campsite was in the lovely valley

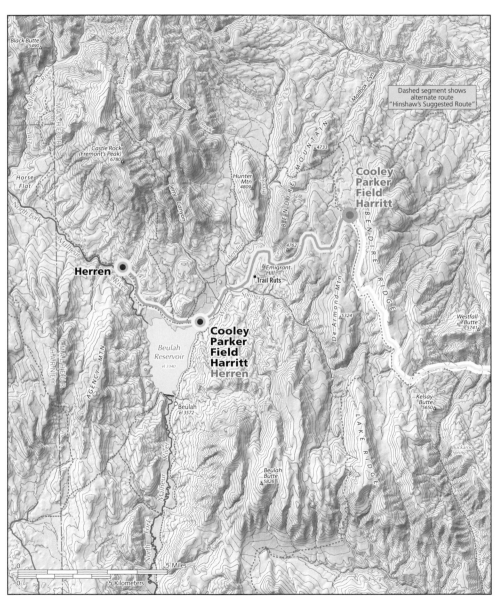

MAP 15 August 30, 1845

A cultivated section of the valley further upstream on the North Fork of the Malheur River.

Valley where Herren and the other diarists probably camped. Beulah Reservoir is in the background.

along the North Fork of the Malheur. Erosion and cultivation have long erased any traces of ruts or a camp and our metal detectors revealed nothing. Upriver toward Castle Rock, there is a natural exit from the valley before the valley becomes an impassable gorge. We also walked part of that route, but found nothing. The trail leads to the Castle Rock Ranch several miles upriver where we found ruts and a grave.

The four other diarists continued to trail Herren and camped at Herren's August 29 campsite. All but Parker comment favorably on the good grass and water. Parker writes, "Rock all day pore grass more swaring then you ever heard."

Field, Harritt, and Cooley, traveling about a day behind Herren, report on August 31 that they camped that day on a stream affording plenty of water and grass. Fremont's Peak, now known as Castle Rock, had been in sight since Westfall Butte and was now looming above Herren.

Field, on August 31, camping near Herren's August 30 site, writes, "We camped once more on Malheur River near a peak in the Blue Mts. called Fremont's Peak, the highest point of land in this part of the country, and easily distinguished at a great distance by a large conical rock upon its summit, having one perpendicular side. . . . Found an excellent encampment again here."

John C. Fremont's expedition may have seen this peak in October 1843, but no one knows how Field, traveling two years later, made the identification.

Cooley also notes "a verry high mountain" in his diary entry of August 31.

HERREN: *This morning very wet and rainy, late breakfast. 9 o'clock before we collected our oxen together, 10 o'clock all of the wagons on the roll again. Traveled about 5 miles a west course to the stream that we left the 26th. Here we encamped for there are mountains all around us, and we have the Blue Mountains to climb over again to-morrow that are said to be 25 miles across. Grass very good and plenty of Willows, Alder, and Balm on the mountains. Some cedar, but they are small and low; the mountains where we are now are covered with grass; it grows up under the snow in winter and dries up with the heat of summer, but does not rot like it would farther east where it rains through summer, for it seldom ever rains here in the summer. The cattle and horses eat it as well as they would well cured hay. Wild sage growing. Scarce 100 miles from Boise river.*

Looking west toward Castle Rock.

PARKER: *Rock all day   pore grass   more swaring then you ever heard   11*

COOLEY: *The road to day has been broken but tolerable good. A sprinkle of rain this evening. Come about West [written in left margin: "Crossed a small branch"] for about 4 miles and struck Mallaer River and camped. Plenty of grass and wood here. Traveled down the creek wee camped on last nite about 1-1/2 and left it on our left. Come to the left of a verry high mountain leaving it on our rite.   4 miles*

FIELD: *Went about 12 miles today, over mountains as high as any yet met with, but some of them were grassy without* rocks, whilst others were covered with big, round stones so nice to jounce wagons over, spoken of back toward Ft. Hall. We camped upon a small branch and found grass and water both plenty and good, which was what our cattle stood in much need of, as for several days we have had hard roads and bad camps, which has cut down stock lower than at any time. Three or four oxen have laid down in the road and given out every day for the past few days.*

HARRITT: *Had a fine shower of rain last night; this morning the fog was so thick that we had great difficulty in collecting our cattle; made a start at 9 o'clock, traveled ten miles over huge mountains, and encamped on Hill Fork,* a beautiful little branch; found good grass and willows; a few rods from us was a warm spring bursting from the side of a lofty mountain, a little above blood heat.*

SUNDAY, AUGUST 31

Herren traveled five miles to Castle Rock Ranch, immediately south of Castle Rock. Harritt, Parker, Field, and Cooley traveled five miles and camped at or near Herren's August 30 site.

- -

HERREN APPARENTLY LEFT THE NORTH FORK OF the Malheur River valley several miles east of what is now known as the Castle Rock Ranch. He took a route north of the river, since an impassable gorge blocked the river route. While we found no identifiable ruts, the trail matched Herren's description of "west over some very steep hills, and some rocks." Field, traveling a day behind, describes the detour around the North Fork as follows: "The road today, for short turns, sidling places, hard pulls, and jolting stones was rather ahead of anything we have had in the same distance, but the camping is first rate."

Herren's description of his August 31 encampment on the north side of the North Fork of the Malheur River matches a description of the now cultivated fields at the base of Castle Rock. He writes that his party "traveled only 5 miles to-day and encamped south of a peak of the mountain that is about 2 miles high. . . . There is on its summit a rock that is about one hundred feet high, and has on its top some beautiful young pine."

The other diarists remained one day behind Herren.

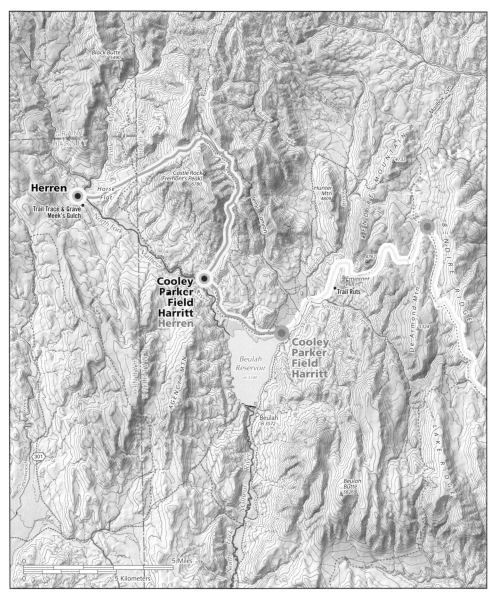

MAP 16 August 31, 1845

Probable route around the North Malheur gorge.

Herren's probable August 31 camp and Castle Rock in the background.

North Fork of the Malheur gorge between Herren's exit point from the river and the Castle Rock Ranch.

We spent part of the day investigating a blind alley. Del Hinshaw's route, as well as other route descriptions, shows the trail traveling up the north side of the North Fork of the Malheur River approximately three miles past today's Castle Rock Ranch house and then crossing the river at that point. After two hours of hiking, we realized that the river was inaccessible both at that point and anywhere near it. Nearly perpendicular walls would have prevented the wagons from getting near the water. While the gorge was spectacular, this route is clearly off the trail. On the other hand, the North Fork of the Malheur River is easily crossed at the Castle Rock Ranch.

HERREN: *Started about 8 o'clock with the expectation of crossing the mountains to-day. 7 oxen were missing, so we had to leave 5 wagons that did not come up with us until 2 o'clock and would not have overtaken us then if we had not laid by for them, so we traveled only 5 miles to-day and encamped south of a peak of the mountain that is about 2 miles high. We could see it five days before we came to it. There is on its summit a rock that is about*

one hundred feet high, and has on its top some beautiful young pine. Our course to-day was about west over some very steep hills, and some rocks. Grass good and plenty of dry willows and Alder.

PARKER: *went up the Creek   5*

COOLEY: *The road to day has been very broken and some rock. Crossed the River this morning & there turned to the rite over the hills and in about 1-1/2 miles come near the River then left it again. Went over the hills. Again here a verry steep hill, then struck the river again and come about 1 mile up it and camped. Plenty of grass and wood here. Weather fine. Freemonts peak.   5 miles*

FIELD: *Went about five miles this morning and camped once more on Malheur River near a peak in the Blue Mts. called Fremont's Peak, the highest point of land in this part of the country, and easily distinguished at a great distance by a large conical rock upon its summit, having one perpendicular side to it. Found an excellent encampment again here.*

HARRIT: *Road tolerable good; made an advance of five miles, and encamped on a stream affording the best of water; grass and timber in abundance.*

MONDAY, SEPTEMBER 1

Herren traveled up "Meek's Gulch," then down Cottonwood Creek, camping in a field that is now part of the Moon Ranch. Harritt, Parker, and Field traced Herren's five-mile climb and descent to his camping site on the North Fork of the Malheur River below Castle Rock. Cooley, his odometer still seeming in error, reported travel of ten miles. His campsite, however, seems to match the descriptions of Field, Harritt, and Parker.

- -

HERREN LEFT HIS CAMPSITE ON THE NORTH FORK of the Malheur River near present day Castle Rock Ranch, traveling up or alongside "Meek's Gulch." Herren's party then crossed to the Cottonwood Creek watershed and traveled down Cottonwood Creek, camping near the present-day site of the Turner Ranch house and a twentieth-century reservoir. (When we visited, it was known as the Turner Ranch. It was formerly known as the Altnow Ranch and is now known as the Moon Ranch.) The other diarists appeared to be a day behind Herren.

Herren's description of trail difficulties is worth noting: "On leaving this stream we traveled up a hollow or gulch that was I expect as rough a way as ever a wagon traveled. We had to remove some ten thousand stones before we could pass near the head of this ravine."

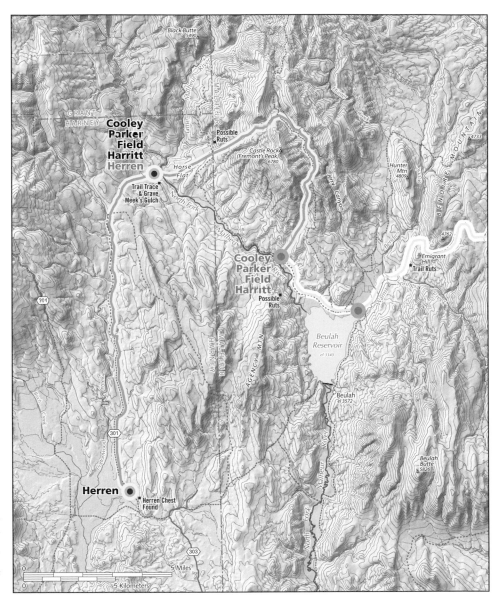

MAP 17 September 1, 1845

Local residents guided us to Meek's Gulch, a rocky ravine a few hundred yards from Herren's August 31 camp. Expedition member Bob Boyd, a personal friend of Del Hinshaw's, says that Hinshaw heard the term "Meek's Gulch" from a neighboring rancher during the 1930s when Hinshaw was working on the Beulah dam. Paul Cronin found ruts leading out of Herren's encampment similar to Herren's diary comments of September 1.

Susie Ragen found a likely gravesite a few yards off the trail leading out of the campsite. The photo shows a headstone, and the center of the grave (under rocks) suspiciously depressed. A metal detector also registered metallic material under the rocks.

The Cottonwood Creek watershed is a stony and inhospitable area. Two or three miles north of the Cottonwood Creek reservoir, we took photos of a protected section of the creek streambed showing a full growth of willows and grasses—probably similar to the terrain in 1845. The contrasting photo of a streambed a few yards from the protected area clearly shows the destructive power of cattle on the environment.

Herren reported that he found grass and willow at the campsite some fifteen miles from Castle Rock Ranch. Traveling down Cottonwood Creek south of the reservoir to the Turner Ranch, Steve Lent found ruts just east of the man-made lake adjacent to the ranch house. They are difficult to discern, but could be remnants of a trail. Del Hinshaw's

trail map and local legend indicate that a chest and other emigrant paraphernalia were abandoned at this campsite. Apparently, the articles were carted off many decades ago.

Herren writes, "I hope that no other emigrants will ever be gulled as we have been." Clearly, the strains associated with taking Meek's route were becoming apparent. In his undated narrative, Samuel Hancock says:

Finally crossing this range of mountains the route became better, being comparatively relieved of these miserable stones so destructive to our teams, although destitute of water; in the hope of reaching water we were now obliged

Meek's Gulch from the air with Castle Rock Ranch in the background.

Meek's Gulch.

Ruts leading out of the August 31 campsite.

Another photo of ruts leading out of the camp on the North Fork of the Malheur River.

Unmarked grave.

Cottonwood Creek.

to urge our exhausted animals forward, and in this effort drove all night when we could. One night thirty of our cows left us, and we did not know but that they were stolen by the Indians, although we had seen nor heard nothing of them since penetrating this miserable country, which seemed almost impervious to the savages even.

Although Hancock does not name a specific time or place, his description probably reflects the emigrant's attitude at this location, his relief at leaving the extraordinarily stony area around Westfall Butte, and growing discontent with Meek's leadership.

HERREN: *Made an early start. 7 o'clock all on the move again, about a southwest course. Soon crossed the little stream called Malheur for the last time I expect that I shall ever see it and unless it was better travelling on its banks than it is, I hope that no other emigrants will ever be gulled as we have been. On leaving this stream we traveled up a hollow or gulch that was I expect as rough a way as ever a wagon traveled. We had to remove some ten thousand stones before we could pass near the head of this ravine. We changed our course to south and turned down a dry hollow about 2 miles to where we found first-rate water. Some took dinner here, and then continued our course south down the branch about 1 mile, then we began to climb the mountains again, passed over some very high ones, until late in the evening we came*

Restricted area.

A nearby area open to grazing.

Possible ruts east of the reservoir at the Turner Ranch.

into a valley and passed through it to a small stream running southwest, and encamped about half past six; found plenty of grass and some dry willow. Distance to-day 15 miles.

PARKER: *the worst Road you ever seen   5 wagons Broak   Missis But Wors [Mrs. Butts worse]   17*

COOLEY: *Weather fine to day. Road verry rough and broken. Crossed the creek this morning and come up a hollow which is verry rockey. Come about 4 miles and struck a branch - only water in holes. Come about 1 mile down it and after crossing it 3 times left it to our left and turned up a hollow and in about 5 miles further struck a branch and camped. Plenty of grass and willow here. Plenty of wood and grass on the branch wee crossed 3 times. The corse has been a little West of South.   10 miles*

FIELD: *Went about 5 miles, camping again on the Malheur. The road today, for short turns, sidling places, hard pulls, and jolting stones was rather ahead of anything we have had in the same distance, but the camping is first rate.*

HARRITT: *Made a small move of five miles over a bad road and encamped on the same stream opposite Fremont's Peak, one of the loftiest points of the Blue Mountains; found good grass and alder timber in abundance.*

Herren's probable September 1 camping site. Many decades ago, an abandoned chest was reportedly found in these fields. The reservoir is a new feature. In 1845, slow-flowing Cottonwood Creek drained this terrain.

TUESDAY, SEPTEMBER 2

Herren, covering twelve miles, camped several miles beyond Drewsey on the O'Toole Ranch. Harritt, Parker, and Field apparently followed Herren's track, camping on the Turner (Moon) Ranch. It appears likely that Cooley was with Harritt, Parker, and Field. His diary record leaves room for uncertainty.

HERREN TRAVELED SEVEN MILES SOUTH TO THE Middle Fork of the Malheur River near Drewsey and then turned west. He apparently camped about one mile west of what is now the O'Toole Ranch homesite. His total recorded distance of twelve miles for the day places his campsite on a flat, grassy area with little other vegetation. Today, cattle grazing has denuded the site of willows and grasses.

Harritt's, Field's, and Parker's descriptions of the rough road out of the North Fork of the Malheur River campsite suggests that they continued a day behind Herren. Field writes, "About 4 miles of our road this morning rather exceeded anything we have passed over yet for rock, they being both large and sharp, lying in a narrow ravine where there was no shunning them." Parker simply noted "the worst you ever seen a wagon gow." Harritt also comments on the terrible road "bad roads for two miles; broke an axletree, which detained us about two hours."

Cooley's route is more difficult to determine. It is likely he was traveling near the others, but his

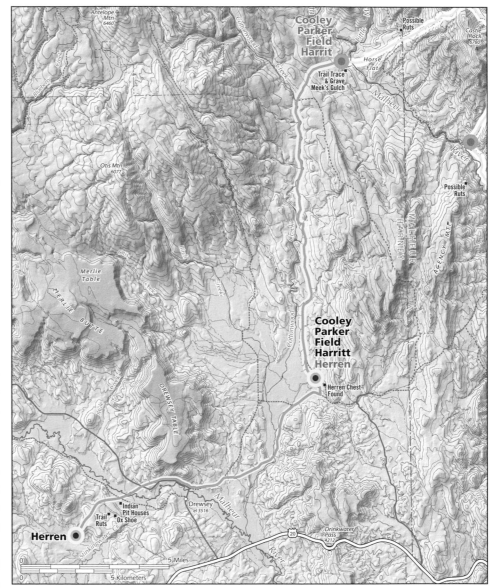

MAP 18 September 2, 1845

Herren likely camped along this creek on September 2. The O'Toole Ranch can be seen in the upper left corner. The pond in the foreground was not present in 1845.

Probable Herren campsite on the O'Toole Ranch.

September 2 diary entry is unclear; his description of the terrain covered does not seem to correlate well with those of the other diarists. Perhaps he lagged behind or was ahead of the others by a few miles.

At the O'Toole Ranch, about two miles northeast of Drewsey, Pat O'Toole called our attention to several artifacts, including an ox shoe, he had found on the portion of the Meek Trail that traversed his ranch. He also showed us depressions in the ground that he believed were the bottom part of a Northern Paiute Indian dwelling. Steve Lent referred to them as Indian pit houses. Pit houses, built by Indians living on the plateau, were partially subterranean dwellings. Wooden beams were laid over a shallow hole in the earth and the frame was then covered with reeds, skins, earth, or possibly stone. Incidentally, some accounts of the Blue Bucket gold discovery associate the discovery date and location with Indian stone huts. The depressions are near the trail and the huts would have been clearly visible by the emigrants. Today, the pits are within a hundred yards of the O'Toole homestead.

Pat O'Toole learned of the 1845 trail from an old sheepherder he employed years ago. The sheepherder said that he had come to what is now the O'Toole Ranch when he was about ten years old, accompanying his father, who was driving a freight wagon. While waiting to meet another wagon from California, the herder and his father camped out and traveled along ruts that the father described as the Meek Cutoff.

O'Toole then drove us to the trail. The ruts were clearly evident in the sagebrush. The line of the ruts was straight and headed west through the sagebrush. The outriders always tried to locate the trail in a straight line and on ground as flat as possible, as the wagons were top-heavy and unstable and tended to tip over on curves.

During the afternoon, Margi Heater, with her metal detector, found an ox shoe nail and, later, an actual ox shoe, right on the trail. It confirmed that we were on track.

Examining Meek artifacts at the O'Toole Ranch.

Eroded trail ruts southwest of the O'Toole Ranch house.

Remnants of Indian pit houses on the O'Toole Ranch.

Ox shoes from the trail on the O'Toole Ranch.

HERREN: *Started about 8 o'clock and traveled about a south course 7 miles to the south branch of Malheur, and waited for one wagon that had the tongue broken out of it.   2 o'clock wagon up with the company. Here we turned a southwest course to a branch of the same stream we left at noon. It had nearly dried up. Grass very good on its banks, and a few willows. Our road in the forenoon was very good, but in the afternoon the route was very hilly and stone. The mountains still continue covered with grass and some scrubby cedar, but a tree three feet in diameter will not be over twenty-five feet high. The country appears to be getting more level. Distance to-day about 12 miles.*

PARKER: *went to A Small Creek down the worst you ever seen a wagon gow   stony   10*

COOLEY: *The road to day has been broken. Weather fine. Crossed the branch this morning and traveled about South for about 5 miles and struck a creek and traveled up it a short distance and crossed it then left it to our rite and in about 5 miles struck a Drean of the creek and camped. The drean has only water in holes. Plenty of grass and willow on the creek and also here the road for about 7 miles is clear of rock; then is some what rockey to the bottom of the drean on which wee camped.   10 miles*

FIELD: *Traveled about 15 miles today, in a direction but little west of south, camping upon a small branch of the Malheir which puts into the South fork. About 4 miles of our road this morning rather exceeded anything we have passed over yet for rock, they being both large and sharp, lying in a narrow ravine where there was no shunning them. We got through, however, with only one broken axel-tree and two wagon-tongues, together with some other little fixings, which was really a favorable come-off.*

HARRITT: *Made an early start, over bad roads for two miles; broke an axletree, which detained us about two hours; balance of the road tolerably good; traveled twelve miles, and encamped on a small rivulet winding its way through a level valley, with its margin beautifully adorned with small willows.*

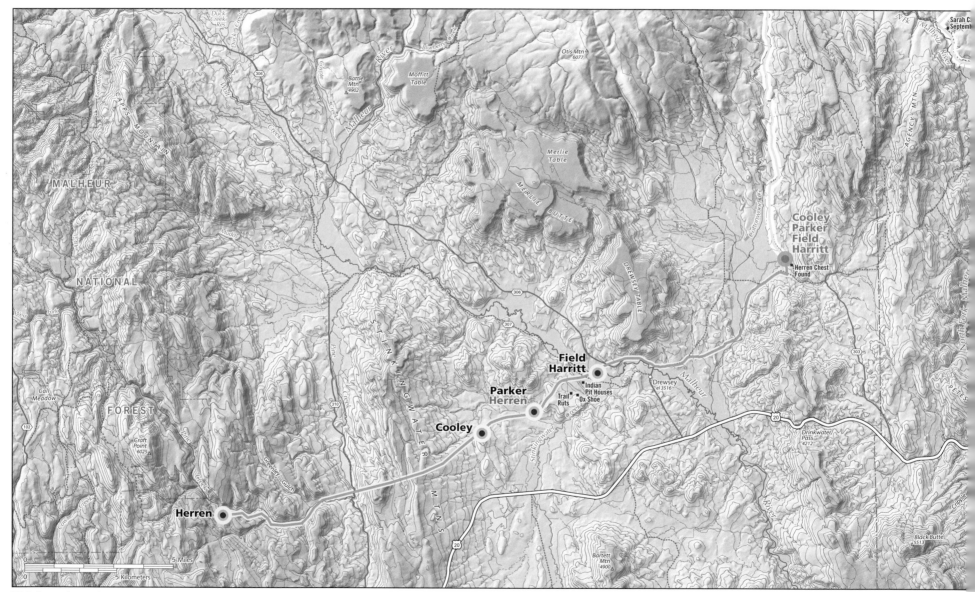

MAP 19 September 3, 1845

Herren traveled ten miles and probably camped on Little Pine Creek. Harritt, Parker, Field, and Cooley continued a day behind Herren.

AFTER TRAVELING TEN MILES, HERREN PROBABLY camped on or near Little Pine Creek. We have no basis for questioning Del Hinshaw's September 3 site location since the place was fenced and inaccessible to us. Herren's description of the route and the creek, however, matches the general area as we traveled around it and then viewed it from the air. Harritt, who reached the campsite one day later, writes: "Encamped in a deep hollow out of which proceeded a number of fine springs, affording us good water as ever run, with a few small willows."

The diaries of Harritt, Field, and Cooley suggest that they were still one day behind Herren and probably camped at his September 2 site. Parker may or may not have been with them. While trailing Herren, Parker's description of a stony road suggests he was not exactly with Harritt, Field, and Cooley.

In an aerial view, the trail leading west from the September 2 campsite on the O'Toole Ranch is clearly visible in the sagebrush.

A mile or two west of the September 2 campsite the trail ascends a rise where we saw and photographed stones apparently moved by the emigrants so that they could travel over the hill.

The reader can imagine the emigrants' emotions as they looked east over the inhospitable area just traveled to see the one recognizable topographical landmark, Fremont's Peak, fading into the dusk. The hardships of the day-to-day routine were clearly becoming more difficult. W. A. Goulder, in his reminiscence, describes the emigrants' attitude as they moved west:

The people who have their homes in that region now have been able to trace our devious and painful track, and wonder why we kept so far away from water, and why we chose a pathway so beset with difficulties of every kind. It was simply because we were bewildered and lost, and acted as people always do under similar circumstances. With men ahead on horseback, looking out for a possible camping-place, the train of wagons would be kept moving all the long day, and often into the darkness of night. The men ahead would build huge beacon fires of sage-brush. Whenever one of those lighted up away off in the front, everybody with the train would indulge the hope that the long looked-for camping-ground, with water, had been found. The process would be kept up until away into the night, with the necessity, almost sure to come, that we would at last be obliged to stop from mere exhaustion and make our camp without grass or water.

An aerial view of the possible Pine Creek campsite.

The trail west from the September 2 campsite on the O'Toole Ranch.

Two hundred yards up the trail from the bottom photograph on the preceding page.

An aerial view of the trail through the sagebrush on the O'Toole Ranch.

A close-up of the trail on the O'Toole Ranch. The arrows mark the remnants of the trail ruts. This view, from a slightly different perspective, encompasses the upper right quarter of the photograph above right.

Stones just to the right of the trail.

Looking east from the trail toward Castle Rock in the far distance.

By September 3, the emigrants were beginning to lose confidence in Meek. Herren writes: "We are rather doubtful that our pilot is lost for he has been seven days longer getting to the waters of Jay's river than he told us he would be. Some talk of stoning and others say hang him. I cannot tell how the affair will terminate yet, but I will inform you in its proper place."

Looking east from the O'Toole ranch, we could clearly see Castle Rock far in the distance behind us. We wondered how the emigrants felt at that time. The distinct peak that had been in sight for several days was behind them and falling below the horizon. In front was an inhospitable and rocky terrain with no end in sight.

A DEATH ON THE TRAIL

Sarah Chambers died on September 3 and was buried on a knoll near the north bank of the North Fork of the Malheur River. The site is some five days behind Herren's lead position. Hinshaw's diary annotations place the Chambers party with Tetherow. The location and date of the burial site shows how widely separated the train had become. Clearly, Sarah was traveling with a nondiarist company of the 1845 train.

The inscription and the gravesite are deeply moving. Sarah Chambers's grave is the only marked and named gravesite on the entire trail from Vale to the Deschutes River.

The inscription on the headstone reads: "Mrs. S. Chambers, Sept. 3d 1845." The plaque reads:

Sarah King Chambers

Sarah King Chambers was born July 25, 1823, in Madison County, Ohio, to Naham and Serepta King.

In the spring of 1845, she, along with her husband, Rowland, and their children Margaret and James, joined other members of the King family on their migration west. Their destination was the Willamette Valley of Oregon, for a new beginning in a land which held great promise.

With about 1,000 other emigrants and 200 wagons, the King party chose to follow Stephen Meek in an ill-fated attempt to cross central Oregon on their way to the upper Willamette Valley, near present-day Eugene. Meek convinced them that this new route would avoid many hazards of the Blue Mountains, the restless Cayuse Indians, and the perilous journey down the Columbia River.

Their group became known as the "Lost Wagon Train of 1845." Not really lost, but desperate for water in these high deserts, they abandoned their plans for a new route and turned north toward the Columbia River and the established trail to Oregon. They arrived at the mission in The Dalles in October in a most deplorable condition.

Sarah Chambers's headstone.

Sarah Chambers's gravesite.

An aerial view of Sarah Chambers's grave.

Sarah could not complete that journey. She died on September 3, 1845, and was buried here, alongside the "Terrible Trail." The cause of death was not recorded in contemporary accounts.

There were twenty-three other known deaths along the cutoff route from where they left the Oregon Trail at the crossing of the Malheur River (in present-day Vale, Oregon) until they rejoined the Oregon Trail at the Mission at The Dalles.

Research, Funding, and Signing by the Oregon-California Trails Association

1991

An article from the *Oregonian* of October 5, 1950, titled "Pioneer Woman's Mystery Solved by Grandchildren," adds the information that Sarah's husband, Rowland Chambers, was "a substantial citizen, who came west with the Kings in 1845, settled in King's Valley [Benton County] and established what descendants believe was Oregon's first grist mill there in 1855." Records maintained by the family "indicate that Chambers started his westward trek in a wagon drawn by two oxen. When one died, he hitched a cow—one of 35 blooded Durhams he brought with him—in its place."

A letter by Stephen and Mariah King written from Oregon on April 1, 1846, talks about the medical problems that affected their family during the journey, particularly while on the Meek Cutoff:

I wrote to you from Fort Larima [Laramie] that the whooping cough and measles went through our camp, and after we took the new route a slow, lingering fever prevailed . . . listen to the deaths: Sally Chambers [the writer is probably referring to Sarah Chambers], John King and his wife, their little daughter Electa and their babe, a son 9 months old, and Dulancy C. Norton's sister are gone. Mr. A. Fuller lost his wife and daughter Tabitha. Eight of our two families have gone to their long homes.

HERREN: *We started this morning about 8 o'clock, and traveled a southwest course over some very rough mountains and rock roads to another branch of the Malheur that afforded us good water and some grass, though not sufficient, and plenty of dry willows for fire wood, and some small cedar. We passed some pine timber to-day. Weather very warm and dry. There is nothing here to cheer our drooping spirits. We are making slow headway; the country here is so broken and rocky that we cannot get along fast, and we are rather doubtful that our pilot is lost for he has been seven days longer getting to the waters of Jay's river than he told us he would be. Some talk of stoning and others say hang him. I can not tell how the affair will terminate yet, but I will inform you in its proper place; 5 miles to-day southwest and 5 miles west. Total to-day, 10 miles. There is considerable cedar on the mountains here, but it is low and has limbs to the ground.*

PARKER: *Stony all day   fore miles you codent See the ground   10*

COOLEY: *The road to day has been verry broken and rockey. Weather fine. Crossed the Drean this morning and have traveled about a South West corse - in about 7 miles crossed a Drean after coming down a verry steep hill. Some grass and wood. Water in holes and in about 1 mile furthur crossed a branch and camped. Some grass and wood here. Some scattering seder on the hills now for about 30 or 40 miles.   8 miles*

FIELD: *Went only about 6 miles today, as we were obliged to put in a new axle-tree. Camped upon the South fork of Malheur again. It is now pretty evident that Meek, the pilot who is leading the company this route instead of the old one, does not intend to fall down to the Columbia via the John Day river at all as he told them on leaving Fort Boise, for we are evidently now through the Blue Mts., and still making a southwest course. It is now said that Meek's intention is to take us over onto the head of the Willamette if he can find a place along the Cascades which will admit of the passage of wagons through, and if not we go down the Deschutes River to the Columbia.*

HARRITT: *Made a new axletree; started late; had good road; traveled seven miles and encamped on the South Fork of the Malheur River; found good grass and willows.*

THURSDAY, SEPTEMBER 4

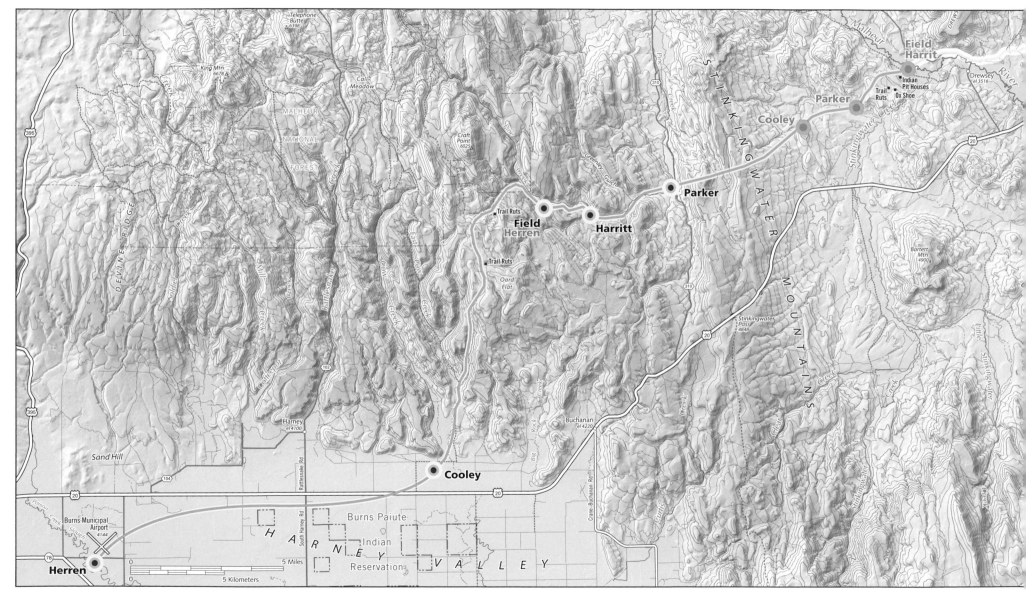

MAP 20 September 4, 1845

Herren traveled fourteen miles, down Rock Creek, then turned west and camped near the present site of the Burns airport. Cooley apparently traveled fourteen miles; his odometer may have malfunctioned. He apparently went down either Rock Creek or East Cow Creek and camped four miles into the Harney Valley. Harritt (eleven miles) and Field (eighteen miles) remained a day behind Herren, camping near Herren's September 3 site. Parker, traveling five miles, camped well short of Harritt and Field.

Possible trail ruts coming out of the Pine Creek campsite.

HERREN LEFT THE PINE CREEK CAMPSITE AND traveled fourteen miles. He apparently camped in the Harney Valley, perhaps near the present site of the Fort Harney Historical Monument. Jack Smith, a local rancher who owns the Cow Creek watershed, led us to a well-traveled trail coming out of the Pine Creek watershed. Mr. Smith said he would "wager a good sum of real money that this is the route Meek took out of Pine Creek." In fact the ruts head south to Rock Creek, where we believe that some of the pioneers went over the hills and down to the Harney Valley. Smith explained that many parts of the Meek route were subsequently used by others, which might explain why some of the ruts are still highly visible.

Possible remnants of the trail northeast of Oard Flat.

Aerial view of Oard Flat.

Trail ruts, now just a rock-filled depression, on Oard Flat.

Probable trail ruts coming off Oard Flat. Other wagons likely used this trail in later years.

In 1924, Fred Lockley, an Oregon journalist and amateur historian interested in the Meek Cutoff, interviewed C. A. Sweek, an early Meek Trail explorer, who commented: "In 1881, when I followed the [Meek] trail, I would frequently see on the bunch grass hills deep cuts where the wheels were locked going down into Harney Valley—on Cow Creek."

Dan Toelle, a local rancher and owner of part of the Cow Creek watershed, believes the emigrants came down East Cow Creek. He believes, as do I, that the ruts visible east of the road coming out of Oard Flat represent the original Meek tracks and that that trail goes straight down East Cow Creek.

According to their diaries, Harritt and Field camped in Herren's September 3 site, still a day behind. Cooley traveled fourteen miles, dropping down off the Stinkingwater Mountains and camp-

ing on the Harney Valley floor: "Here the valley appears to [be] perfectly level as far as the eye can reach." Cooley probably camped near Herren. (Cooley's odometer seemed to malfunction often, and written description of travel often does not match his mileage. We tended to locate him by the written description of terrain and scenery.) Parker's location is unknowable; he traveled only five miles "to A Spring."

As the wagons descended the Stinkingwater Mountains on September 3 and 4, several of the diarists reported sighting the Cascade Range. In fact, they mistook Steens Mountain for the range. Steens Mountain, with an altitude of 9,733 feet, is a large fault-block peak located in the southeastern part of Oregon. From a distance it appears to be a mountain range but it is properly described as a small peak. As he camped south of what is now

Highway 20, Herren wrote, "I hope the grumbling will cease now as our course appears to be west and the peak at the mouth of Jay's river, near the Columbia, is visible, and our pilot says it is about one hundred miles distance." Harritt, traveling a day behind, noted "to the west a large valley; to the southwest the Cascade Mountains."

The 1845 wagon train was now thoroughly lost. It was winding slowly west believing Steens Mountain was the Cascade Range. Field's notes of September 6 illustrate the emigrants total confusion, as he writes that they camped on "another fork of Crooked River instead of John Day as stated yesterday, and we are in fact upon the waters of the Deschutes River, and steering direct toward the Cascade Mts. in order to attempt a passage through them . . . if he [Meek] now fails to take us across the Cascades his head will not be worth a chew of tobacco to him."

Harney Valley in the foreground; Steens Mountain in the distance.

Our expedition traveled south on a rough road from Oard Flat toward the Harney Valley, stopping for lunch at a beautiful overlook some three or four miles north of Highway 20. Steens Mountain was clearly visible from our lunch site. We began to understand how the desperate pioneers could mistake the mountain for the Cascade Range.

HERREN: *We started about 8 o'clock and traveled a south course about 4 miles, then turned southwest about 2 miles and passed down a very rocky hill or mountain into the valley of Jay's River, here we turned a west course about 8 miles to a beautiful little rivulet of water but no wood except small willows. Grass is very good. This valley is on the river that we have been looking for the last seven days. I hope the grumbling will cease now as our course appears to be west and the peak at the mouth of Jay's*

river, near the Columbia, is visible, and our pilot says it is about one hundred miles distance. To-day 14 miles.

PARKER: *to A Spring* 5

COOLEY: *Weather fine to day and the road has been broken for a pease and then first rate. Crossed the main divide to day which is about 7 mile from whare wee camped and about 3 miles further to a valley. This far the road is verry broken and rough and some seder and pine timber. After wee got in to the valley the road was first rate to whare wee camped which was on a small drean about 4 miles from whare wee struck the valley. Some willow and plenty of grass. Here as wee come over the divide wee saw the Cascade Mountains at a considerable distance. Here the valley appears to b perfectly level as far as the eye can reach. Saw some Indians here. The corse is about*

South West to day. 14

FIELD: *Went about 18 miles, the latter part of the road being rough and rocky. Camped upon the head of a small branch of the South fork of Malheur. The mountains where we first struck them were naked and perfectly destitute of timber. Near Fremont's Peak we began to see some timber upon them, and since passing that point the hills have all had more or less timber upon them, it being generally low cedar, and on reaching the top of the last hill before descending into the hollow, tall pines appear to crown the hill-tops before us.*

HARRITT: *Made an advance of eleven miles and encamped in a deep hollow out of which proceeded a number of fine springs, affording us good water as ever run, with a few small willows.*

FRIDAY, SEPTEMBER 5

Herren traveled fifteen miles and camped on the Harney Valley floor near Wright's Point. Cooley traveled fifteen miles and must have camped near Herren. Harritt and Field traveled twelve and fifteen miles, respectively, and also camped in the Harney Valley. Parker claimed to have traveled twenty-three miles. He probably caught up with Harritt and Field, one day behind Herren. Parker's odometer very likely malfunctioned.

- -

HERREN TRAVELED FIFTEEN MILES SOUTHWEST across the Harney Valley. Again his comments show how thoroughly lost the pioneers were. He includes both the Crooked and Jay's River (the John Day) as creeks crossed. In fact he was on a fork of the Silvies River, many miles from either the Crooked or the John Day. The Silvies River, named for Antoine Sylvaille, a trapper who worked the area in 1826, runs for about ninety-five miles through Grant and Harney Counties. It flows into Malheur Lake about twenty-five miles southeast of Burns, Oregon. South of U.S. Highway 20, in the area Herren camped, the Silvies watershed is a slow-moving often swampy stream, with numerous tributaries. Herren accurately describes the Harney Valley floor but again described Steens Mountain as the Cascade Range: "We passed over some very

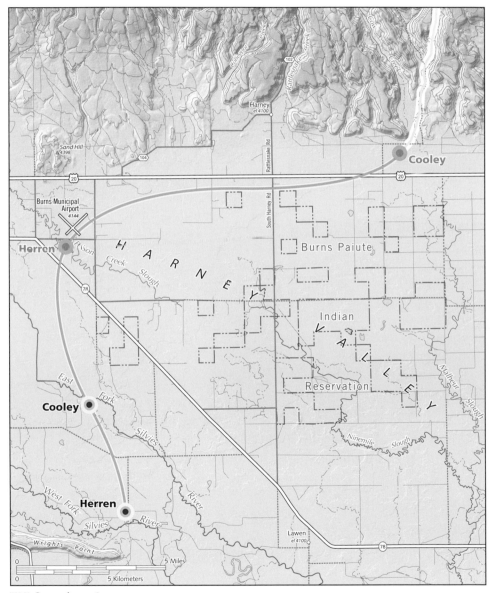

MAP 21 September 5, 1845

One of the many dry creek beds in the Harney Valley basin.

rich looking soil to-day but no timber. This valley is covered with wild sage. The country looks level as far as we can see to the west. We have been in sight of the Cascade mountains for the last twenty miles."

Cooley, also reporting fifteen miles, apparently camped a few miles east of Herren. (In his September 6 diary entry, Cooley reports that he went "3 miles and crossed a small creek," and "about 1 mile further passed the point of a ridge leaving it to the rite.") Cowboys working around the base of Wright's Point told us that local historical lore placed an 1845 emigrant camp near the base of the point. Wright's Point, a basalt mesa, rises about two hundred feet above the Silvies plain. It is the dominant geologic feature south of U.S. Highway 20. As it is located about fifteen miles from the September 4 camp, it appears highly likely that Herren did camp near Wright's Point.

Field and Harritt again were a day behind. Harritt also mistook Steens Mountain for the Cascade

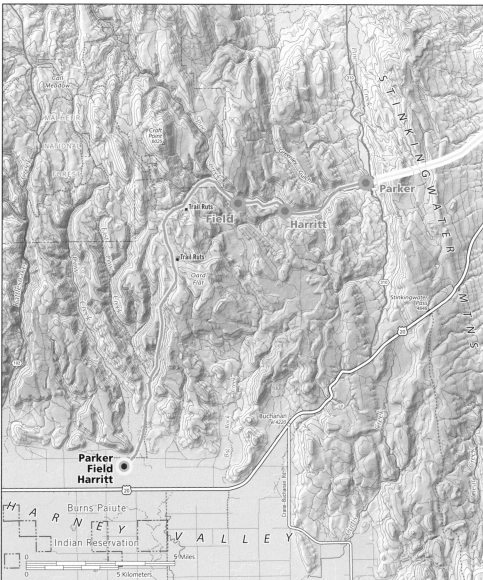

MAP 22 September 5, 1845

The Harney Valley.

Range and Field thought he was on the John Day River. Parker traveled twenty-three miles and apparently caught up with Harritt and Field. His description of "head waters of the digers lakes" must refer to streams flowing into the Silvies River.

We walked parts of the beautiful Harney Valley, but found no trace of ruts. Much of the land is now used for grazing cattle or growing hay. Some of the basin is under irrigation. While over a hundred years of ranching has changed much of the vegetation, in 1845 Herren noted that the valley was covered with "wild sage." In his reminiscence, W. A. Goulder described the scene succinctly: "The new route was a trackless waste, covered, for the most part, by immense fields of sagebrush that grew tall, strong, and dense. Through these sage-fields we were obliged to force the oxen, the teams taking turns ... in breaking their way through the sage. It often consumed a good deal of time in the morning in compelling the oxen to begin their daily task of breaking road."

HERREN: *We started at 8 o'clock and traveled a southwest course across the valley of Crooked or Jay's river, about 15 miles to a branch of Crooked river, which afforded plenty of grass and some fine dry willows for firewood; the water very bad, hardly fit for use. We passed over some very rich looking soil to-day but no timber. This valley is covered with wild sage. The country looks level as far as we can see to the west. We have been in sight of the Cascade mountains for the last twenty miles. The nights are very cold, days pleasant, looks like autumn had set in.*

In the foreground, Herren's probable campsite near the base of Wright's Point.

Farmed land at the base of Wright's Point.

Looking east to Wright's Point. The emigrants came around the rock outcroppings and traveled west toward the photographer.

PARKER: *Crossed the Divide to the head waters of the digers lakes in the nite 11 oclock   23*

COOLEY: *The road to day has been first rate and level. Weather fine. Crossed the drean this morning and left it on our left and have traveled about a South West corse. Crossed a small creek and camped. It runs to the left. Plenty of grass and willow here. Saw a few Indians to day.   15*

FIELD: *Went 15 miles. Camping upon Lake fork of John Day's river. I was mistaken about our being through the main range, yet the road for the past few days has led across low mountains which, having their steepest descent toward the west, did not appear high until we ascended them. The map of the country we had with us also indicated that we had passed the head of the John Day River, as the Malheur was made to head much further south than the John Day, and yet we have held a southwest course from the Malheur, and we are now upon the head forks of the John Day river.*

HARRITT: *As we advanced we gradually ascended a beautiful mountain; gained the top upon which grew a number of pine and cedar trees; a few miles farther a beautiful landscape appeared to sight; to the west a large valley; to the southwest the Cascade Mountains; to the northwest was the Columbia River; we gradually descended this lofty mountain, entered the valley, down which we proceeded five miles; came to a beautiful little rivulet with its banks shaded by a few small willows, where we encamped, having come twelve miles.*

SATURDAY, SEPTEMBER 6

Herren traveled fifteen miles to Harney Lake and then ten miles along its north shore. Cooley traveled eighteen miles, reached the edge of Harney Lake, and camped there. Parker claimed to have traveled twenty-three miles. He probably camped near Field and Harritt, who traveled fourteen miles and camped near Wright's Point.

HERREN LEFT THE CAMP AT WRIGHT'S POINT AND traveled ten miles south around the east side of Dog Mountain and, heading south, reached Harney Lake. He then moved west a few miles, camping at a site without water or wood for a fire, where he nevertheless: "laid down and took a good night's sleep, which revived us considerably." Incidentally, Field, when he reached Harney Lake a day behind Herren, described "a lake of miserable, stagnant water, filled with ducks, geese and cranes, and surrounded with tall rushes, the borders being miry."

Today, Harney Lake probably looks much as it was observed by the emigrants. It is a shallow alkali basin located about thirty miles southeast of Burns and within the boundary of the Malheur National Wildlife Refuge. In normal water years, Harney Lake is barely four feet deep. In drought years, it dries up completely.

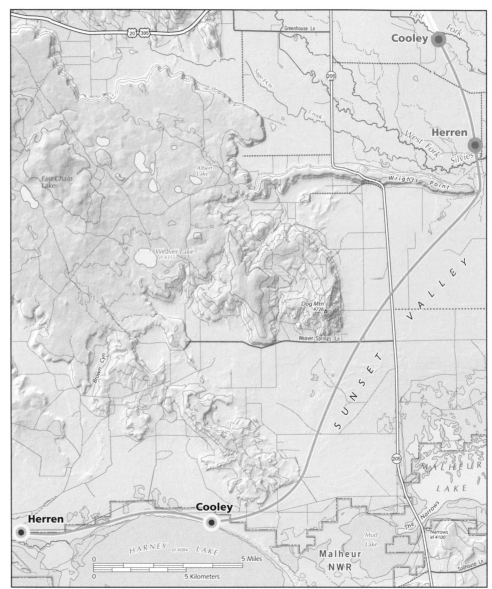

MAP 23 September 6, 1845

A newspaper article from 1867 reported a conversation with Stephen Meek in which Meek describes his long association with Malheur and Harney Lakes:

One great peculiarity of the section of country . . . is the disappearance and re-appearance of a vast lake, sixty miles in length. In 1833 Mr. Meek passed over the identical country, and found the magnificent sheet of water, and actually caught fish and trapped beaver from the same. He was with a train belonging to B. L. E. Bainville [Bonneville] & Co., fur traders of New York. In 1845, when piloting the emigrant train through the wilderness, he found the exact spot where this lake had been—but where no lake then existed. The train of emigrant wagons passed over the spot, which a few years before had been covered by a magnificent sheet of water, and followed through the valley left by the same, sixty miles, to what had been the opposite end of the lake. In 1867 Mr. Meek again returned to the same spot, and imagine his amazement to find the lake as he first witnessed it in 1833—there before him lay the apparently same magnificent sheet of water, looking as beautiful as it did before its entire disappearance. Now, that there may be no doubt of this singular fact, we can produce the evidence of Mr. Meek's own observation. Doubting his own senses he searched the country over until he

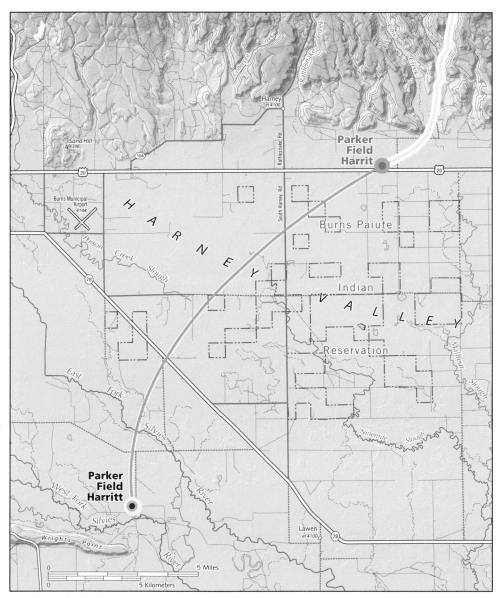

MAP 24 September 6, 1845

Dog Mountain.

An aerial view of the north shore of Harney Lake, July 2009.

found the wagon trail made in 1845, and tracked the same to the end of the lake, where it entered the same (the old track, of course, being covered with the water of the lake mentioned.) He then followed the rim or beach of the lake around to the opposite end, (sixty miles), and there found the wagon trail making its appearance from under the water, and, where twenty-two years before the emigrant train had passed over the self same spot covered now with water. This, to us, and perhaps to the reader, may seem a strange story to relate—but our old citizens know Mr. Meek, and know that they can rely upon his statements.

In *The Brazen Overlanders of 1845,* citing information from hydrologists and geologists, Donna Wojcik describes the fluctuations in size of Malheur Lake and the extremely dry weather in 1845.

There is ample geologic evidence that Malheur lake, fed by mountain streams to the north . . . filled the whole of Harney Basin in an early geologic period and that the remnants of this former lake now exists in Malheur and Harney lakes. They have fluctuated greatly in size over the surface from season to season and year to year. Since 1895, when attention was first seriously given them, these lakes have covered areas in square miles ranging from one-hundred-twenty-five down to two. Neither lake has a boundary nor drainage outlet and both dissipate water by evaporation. One water survey chart of Harney Basin based on tree ring growth from 1735–1935 shows the year 1833 at about 25% below normal precipitation, rising to about 10% above normal until 1835 then declining steadily until 1845, when it reached 41% below normal. In 1867 the chart shows it had

again risen and was about 30% above normal precipitation. Hence the Malheur, fed by mountain streams, had pushed its waters far to the north when Meek first saw it, had disappeared by 1845 and was again in flood stage in 1867 when Meek saw it again; Meek's coming out on Rattlesnake creek in 1845 put him on the west side of the high rise which would have been the western boundary of the lake he expected to find.

Some historians have claimed that the 1845 train traveled north when it reached Harney Lake. In "Cutoff Fever, IV," their September 1977 *Oregon Historical Quarterly* article, Leah Collins Menefee and Lowell Tiller address this issue: "The diary of James Field . . . indicates that at the Silvies there was discussion about passing the lakes on the south side rather than on the north. Stephen Meek, the guide, had recommended the south side, but those with him refused to follow this route and the train crossed the Silvies and moved on south, then west from that stream along the northern edge of the lakes."

The 1845 diaries clearly show that the Meek Cutoff party traveled along the north shore of Harney Lake.

The 1853 Elliott party, traveling roughly in Meek's tracks from Vale to the Harney Valley, turned south at the Malheur and Harney Lake areas and traveled south around the lakes. The reason or reasons for that decision are not known but Menefee and Tiller comment, "It was a detour which took unnecessary days of travel, wore the oxen down even further and resulted in the use of precious provisions. Had the travelers remained on Meeks tracks and passed north of the lakes . . . they would have reached the Deschutes River at least a week sooner."

Field's entry for this date confirms our belief that Field and probably Harritt had been and remained a day behind Herren: "[Meek] is with Owensby's company which is one day's travel ahead of ours, and we make their camps every evening, where we find a note buried at the foot of a stake, stating the distance to the next camp, and the names of the streams."

Cooley traveled eighteen miles, camping near Herren. His notes confirm the dearth of wood at the campsite. Field and Harritt camped near Wright's Point. Parker, who again claimed to travel twenty-three miles, appeared to be ahead of Field and Harritt.

HERREN: *We started about 7 o'clock and traveled about south 15 miles. Here we came to a lake which caused us to turn to the west about 10 miles; trying to get water we traveled until about 8 o'clock at night, and encamped without wood, water, fire or supper, or anything to console us, so we laid down and took a good night's sleep, which revived us considerably. 176 miles from Boise river.*

PARKER: *down the Botom Sandy and Sage 23*

COOLEY: *The road to day is first rate. Weather fine. Come about 3 miles and crossed a small creek. Plenty of grass and willow here on the creek. In about 1 mile further passed the point of a ridge leaving it to the rite and in about 14 miles further camped by a lake. Leaving it to the left the creek runs to the left. Plenty of grass, no wood, some sage here. The corse has been a little West of South. 18 miles*

FIELD: *Went about 14 miles today, camping upon another fork of Crooked River instead of John Day as stated yesterday, and we are in fact upon the waters of the Deschutes River, and steering direct toward the Cascade Mts. in order to attempt a passage through them. The tale of our going down the John Day river was a mere tale of Meek's in order to get us upon this route and then take us wherever he pleased. But if he now fails to take us across the Cascades his head will not be worth a chew of tobacco to him, if what some of our men say prove true. He is with Owensby's company which is one day's travel ahead of ours, and we make their camps every evening, where we find a note buried at the foot of a stake, stating the distance to the next camp, and the names of the streams.*

HARRITT: *Continued down this rich valley fourteen miles and encamped on Crooked River, a small murmuring stream running to the south, shaded on its banks by a few willows. As we advanced this morning the beautiful scenery increased; this valley is one of the most sublime places I ever saw; it is from appearances from thirty to fifty miles wide from north to south, the length of which I am not able to determine; the soil is rich and beautifully set with fine grass, intermingled with patches of sage; the mountains to the north in places are thinly set with pine and cedar timber.*

SUNDAY, SEPTEMBER 7

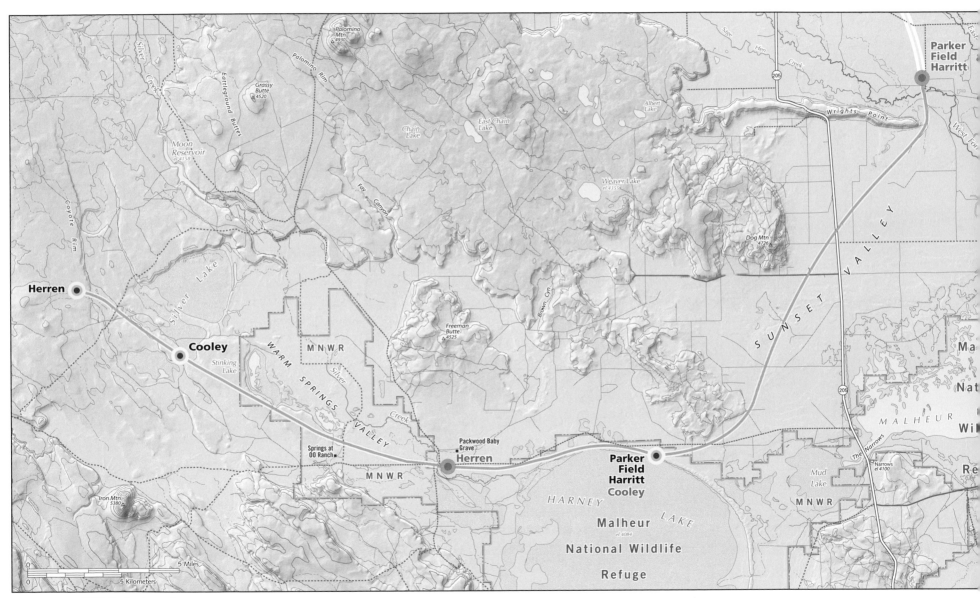

MAP 25 September 7, 1845

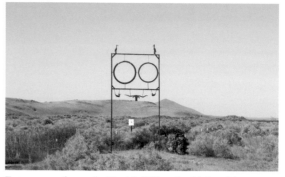

Entrance marker at the Double O Ranch with Iron Mountain in the background.

A spring on the Double O Ranch.

A spring on the Double O Ranch.

Herren traveled fifteen miles, past Silver Lake, and camped on a creek a few miles west of the lake. Harritt and Field both traveled sixteen miles, and Parker claims twenty-two miles. Again, despite his stated mileage, it is likely Parker traveled with Harritt and Field. While the three diarists reached Harney Lake, Cooley traveled some ten miles ahead, west along Harney Lake, and probably camped near its northwest corner.

- -

HERREN AGAIN TRAVELED FIFTEEN MILES MOVING west, and we are certain that he reached a creek west of Silver Lake, which he describes as "a small stream of water about ten feet wide and nearly as many feet deep; water good and grass first-rate; no wood only sage." All of the diarists probably camped at or near this or other springs a day or two after Herren.

Cooley traveled along the shore of Harney Lake and perhaps reached Silver Lake. Harritt, Field, and Parker, still a day behind Herren, reached Harney Lake and camped on its north shore. Each of their diary entries for September 7 confirms reaching a lake. From their line of travel, the location had to be Harney Lake.

The cold spring we visited on the Double O Ranch, now within the boundaries of the Malheur National Wildlife Refuge, is about two or three miles northwest of the ranch house. The spring is surrounded by sagebrush, with neither trees nor willows to mark it. It is perhaps two hundred to four hundred feet long. The spring is a foot to several feet deep and is surrounded by tall grass.

To visit the spring we left a very rough dirt road and walked a half to three-quarters of a mile through sagebrush and alkali flats. The temperature was over ninety degrees Fahrenheit. The vegetation was mainly sagebrush with not a tree in sight. This short hike gave us a feel for the emigrants' trek across this part of eastern Oregon, lost, with minimal water in intense heat, walking over rocky and scrub soil surrounded by wagons, cattle, goats, horses, and dust.

The spring we visited was just one of several in the area. In my opinion, the emigrants could have camped anywhere in the general vicinity. We found no signs of a trail.

HERREN: *We started at 7 o'clock and traveled through a poor, sandy valley 14 miles to a small stream of water about ten feet wide and nearly as many feet deep; water good and grass first-rate; no wood only sage. Course today west. Distance 15 miles.*

PARKER: *Struck the lakes   Bad water   22*

COOLEY: *The road to day has been good. Weather fine. Come about 10 miles and struck a creek and camped. Plenty of grass and willow here. The creek runs to the left and thrugh the lake and then round to the rite in to Jays river round the mountains. Wee left holes to the rite and left. The corse has been about South West or near so. Traveled allmost towards a high point or peak and to the rite is and other some distance off. Crossed a small drean just befor it.*

FIELD: *Went about 16 miles, camping upon a lake of miserable, stagnant water, filled with ducks, geese and cranes,*

An aerial view of some of the springs on the Double O Ranch. Iron Mountain is in the background; Wagontire Mountain is the low-lying mountain to the right of Iron Mountain.

and surrounded with tall rushes, the borders being miry. Had excellent grass but were obliged to pack wormwood for half a mile for fuel. During the night 15 head of horses and mules left us.

HARRITT: *Road beautiful and level, traveled sixteen miles; crossed one small stream and encamped on the margin of a large lake; had an abundance of fine grass; no wood except sage.*

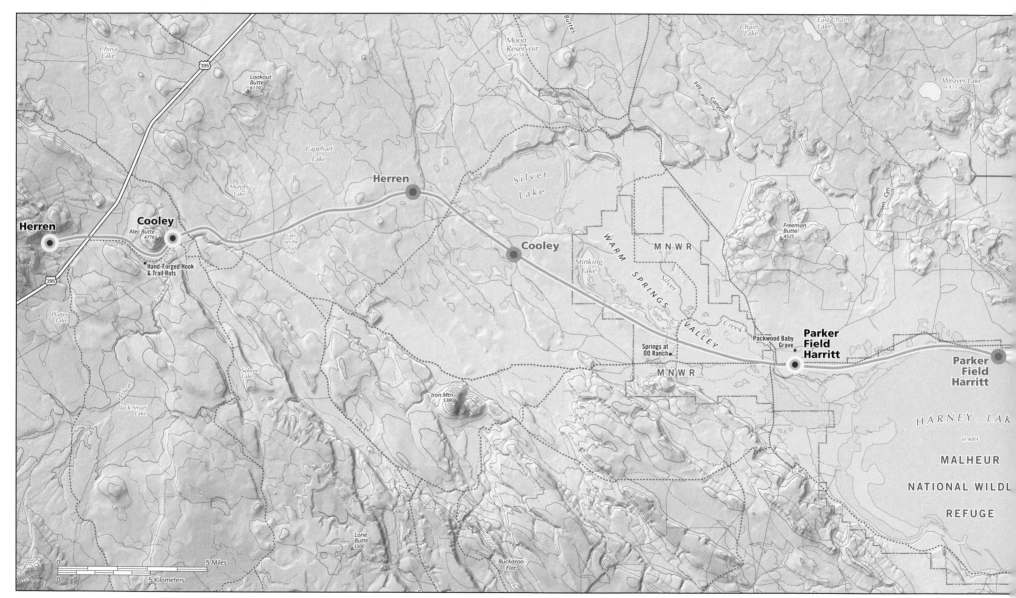

MAP 26 September 8, 1845

The Packwood grave is probably somewhere on this landscape. Iron Mountain is visible in the distance.

Herren traveled fifteen miles, probably to a site just west of what is now Highway 395. Cooley traveled eleven miles and probably camped near Alec Butte. Field (thirteen miles) and Harritt (ten miles) camped west of the west end of Harney Lake. Parker (fifteen miles) had to be with Field and Harritt since he refers to the dead child buried at the camp.

- -

HERREN AGAIN TRAVELED FIFTEEN MILES WEST across desolate alkali plains, perhaps to a site a few miles west of what is now Highway 395. Herren himself comments that the last five miles were rocky road and that his campsite in sagebrush was without grass and with very little water. Field's diary of September 10 notes that Herren's campsite on the eighth was seven miles west of Field's September 9 campsite at or near the Double O springs. So we can locate Herren's September 8 site with some accuracy.

Herren's diary ends on this date. The remaining pages of the diary were mutilated after the September 8 entry and the entire diary was lost in a fire at Heppner, Oregon, on July 4, 1918. If the original still existed, today's technology might have been able to reveal the rest of the diary. Even the word "gold" associated with a date would have sent our expedition members scrambling. Ben Walker (whose identity is unknown) transcribed the four legible pages of the Herren diary, which were later published in the *Albany Daily Democrat*, January 1–2, 1891.

It is absolutely certain that Field, Harritt, and Parker camped together since all three refer to the death of a small child at the September 8 campsite. In his diary entry of September 9, Field writes, "Last evening a child of E. Packwood [Clark and Tiller give the baby's name as Elkanah], of Illinois, which had been ill a few days died suddenly. . . The child was buried in the dry wormwood barrens, and as we left the camp the wagons filed over the grave, thus leaving no trace of its situation." Del Hinshaw locates that site on Silver Creek near the west end of Harney Lake. The site corresponds to the distances each traveled on September 8. Cooley, although he does not note the Packwood death, probably camped slightly west of the other three diarists. Cooley recorded a distance of eleven miles versus ten for Harritt, fifteen for Parker, and thirteen for Field. Since we know that Harritt, Parker, and Field camped together, the difference in mileage probably reflects the inaccuracy of mid-nineteenth century odometers or possibly different routes.

The alkali flats west of Double O Ranch encompass much of the terrain around Silver Lake, perhaps the campsite of one or several companies of the 1845 train. Silver Lake is flat and dry. Its lakebed, about twenty-five or thirty feet below the rim, is covered with sagebrush and alkali deposits.

Alkali Flat.

Silver Lake.

An aerial photograph looking east toward Silver Lake in the distance. The emigrants traveled across these flats toward the photographer.

Few Oregonians have seen Silver Lake and probably most of those who have visited it are not eager to return. The dry, inhospitable stretch of terrain from Harney Lake to Wagontire Mountain is as difficult and remote as any area the pioneers traveled.

HERREN: *We started at 8 o'clock and traveled west about 10 miles over some of the best road that we have had since we passed the Rocky Mountains, but in the evening we had some rocky road for a few miles; here we turned about two degrees north of west for about 5 miles and found no grass and had to encamp in a patch of wild sage, where it was as high as our wagons. About one mile south of where we are we found a little water, enough to cook supper with. The stream of water that we stayed on last night runs out of the side of a mountain through a hole about six feet in diameter; there is water enough within six feet of where it runs out to drown a horse. Passed some plains to-day that were covered . . .*

N. B.—Here the diary was torn and mutilated so that I could not proceed with it any farther.

No. of miles traveled, 210. 226 miles from Boise river. 40 miles west of Harney Lake.
—Ben Walker

PARKER: *went down the lakes some 5 miles then over the hills to A Small Creek   one child buried here   15 miles*

COOLEY: *The road to day has been good except one little rockey place. Weather fine. Traveled up the creek around the head of it. Towards the peak the creek runs along by the side of a bluff and we come along by the point of the bluff leaving it to the left. Here at the point of the bluff is a exealent spring. Some grass, no wood except sage. Then on about a South west corse and by the point of another bluff leaving it to the rite then on near the peak leaving it to the left then on to another high bluff or bench and camped. No water here though we found some water in a hole to the left up a hollow which was sufficient for cooking. Here some of the oxen was tied up all night; others left out. Those that was left out went back to the spring from whare wee camped last nite. To the spring is about 5 miles. From the spring to whare wee lay at nite is about 6.   11 miles*

FIELD: *Went about 13 miles, camping upon a creek which appears to feed the lake our last camp was upon. We have been traveling for the last three days across a nearly dead level plain, in a southwesterly direction, and are now nearly across it, the bluffs arising abruptly from the edge of the plain, which they surround, and are in many places nearly perpendicular. Many parts of this plain, particularly where we struck it, has soil of good depth and is covered with a very fine kind of grass resembling blue grass. Much of it is covered with that same eternal wormwood mentioned so often, and there are many places that look as though they were covered with water during the wet season, now presenting a surface of naked white clay encrusted in places with a white substance resembling saleratus [sodium or potassium bicarbonate used as a leavening agent; baking soda] and answering the same purpose, as some of the women in the camp have proven by experiment. Four of the horses which left our camp were found today at a distance of several miles from it, but there is no news of the others. They probably strayed off in search of water as the borders of the lake were so miry they could not get a drink.*

HARRITT: *Road sometimes delightful; had ten horses stolen last night by the Indians; traveled ten miles, and encamped on a small stream affording good grass and a few small willows; a dreadful occurrence, a few minutes after we were in camp—the sudden death of an infant by that disease which had been fatal before in our company—the whooping cough.*

TUESDAY, SEPTEMBER 9

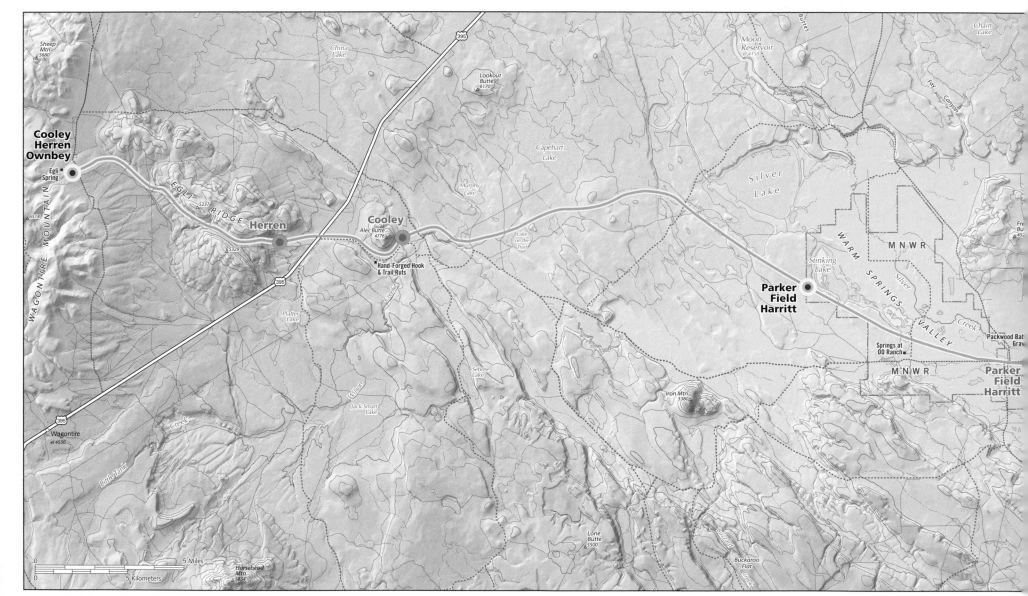

MAP 27 September 9, 1845

From Alec Butte looking east toward Iron Mountain and Silver Lake. On September 8–10, the pioneers took this route across the alkali flats toward Alec Butte, with the likely trail running below the butte on the right side of the photograph.

Ruts south of Alec Butte.

Herren (with Ownbey) probably traveled some ten or twelve miles and camped at Egli Spring. Cooley traveled fifteen miles with or near Herren and camped at Egli Spring. Harritt and Field traveled six miles to springs on today's Double O Ranch. Parker claimed he traveled nine miles but probably was with or near Field and Harritt.

- -

ALTHOUGH HERREN'S DIARY WAS UNDECIPHERable after September 8, his September 9 location can be determined from comments in Field's diary of September 10. Herren was traveling with Ownbey's company. Field, on September 10, noted that when he arrived that evening at a spring he found Ownbey's group, which had arrived 24 hours before on September 9. The site, according to Del Hinshaw, was Egli Spring on the east side of Wagontire Mountain. Since the Egli Spring site roughly matches the distance traveled by Field and others, and since the description of the spring in the diaries matches our visual inspection, we are reasonably confident that this site location is accurate.

Cooley apparently was with or near Herren. His diary of September 9 refers to a "corse . . . about west" and camping at a "first rate spring." Moreover, Cooley did not travel at all on September 10 so he must have been resting at Egli Spring with Herren.

Field, on September 9, traveled only six miles, apparently to the springs of the Double O Ranch. Harritt also traveled six miles, probably to the same site. Parker, whose mileage is often suspect, noted he traveled "to A Spring   9." He was probably with Harritt and Field.

Cooley, in his trek to Egli Spring, refers to a "peak" on his right. Cooley's "peak" was probably Alec Butte, a low-lying mountain located two miles east of Highway 395. We climbed Alec Butte and photographed the possible route from just east of Iron Mountain across the alkali flats to the gap on the south side of the butte.

Searching in the gap Steve Lent found a trail where some wagons, perhaps the 1845 emigration, went through the sagebrush. While part of the road was improved many decades ago, the original track is definitely a trace that melds into the improved road.

With metal detectors we found an artifact in the ruts, tending to confirm that the emigrants may have traveled this route. It appeared to be a hand forged hook, suggesting it was made a long time ago. Perhaps it was a hook that could fit on a wagon. After noting the GPS location, we reburied the hook and moved on.

Incidentally, we were excited to find blue and white pottery shards that we speculated might have fallen from a wagon. But, when examined closely, they revealed the word "Japan." It was a good reminder that while we feel confident we have found the 1845 ruts and wagon parts at several sites, absolutely nothing is certain when tracing lost trails.

We then drove along the east side of Wagontire Mountain, stopping to view Egli Ridge to the east. Egli Spring is perhaps half a mile west of the road. It is a beautiful little stream coming out of the mountains that flows into a manmade reservoir on the east side of the road.

PARKER: *went to A Spring   9*

COOLEY: *Some rock to day. Weather fine. Some of the wagons started early this morning though some of them did not get off until 10 o'clock. Come around the bench leaving it 2 of 3 to the rite. Come around and down in to the valley along it for some distance leaving the peak that wee saw to the rite a little to the rite come along and went over a ridge; some seder on it; leaving 2 ridges between us and the peak and about 2 miles thrugh a valley then over another ridge with seder on it. Still laving the peak to the rite then turned to the left leaving the peak nearly*

Ruts melding into a well-traveled dirt road.

Hand-forged hook.

Looking east to Egli Ridge from Egli Reservoir.

The runoff from Egli Spring, about a half mile east of this site, as it reaches the road.

Egli Reservoir on the east side of the road.

Aerial view looking east. Egli Spring is in the foreground, man-made Egli Reservoir in the distance.

behind us for about ½ or 2 mile and camped—to a first rate spring. Plenty of grass and some wood here. The corse is about west. The road should not come so near the first peak nor over the ridge or bench but after leaving the spring the road should turn more to the rite leaving the first peak further to the left and strike across to the rite hand peak leaving it a little to the rite and struck the road again.   15 miles

FIELD: *Last evening a child of E. Packwood, of Illinois, which had been ill a few days died suddenly. At presently there are a good many sick about the camp, the majority of them complaining of fever. The child was buried in the dry wormwood barrens, and as we left the camp the wagons filed over the grave, thus leaving no trace of its situation. The reason for our doing this was that the Indians in this part of the country are very fond of clothing, giving almost anything they posses in order to* obtain it, and fearing that they might disturb the grave after we left, we took the precaution of leaving a beaten road across it. I cannot say that they would do anything to a grave, were they to find one, for we have passed several made by emigrants at various times, and none of them appeared to have been disturbed. Went 6 miles camping near a spring which sinks near where it rises.

HARRITT: *Attended to the burial of the deceased this morning, before we started; made a start at ten o'clock, traveled six miles over a delightful road and encamped at a spring; found no wood and but little grass.*

WEDNESDAY, SEPTEMBER 10

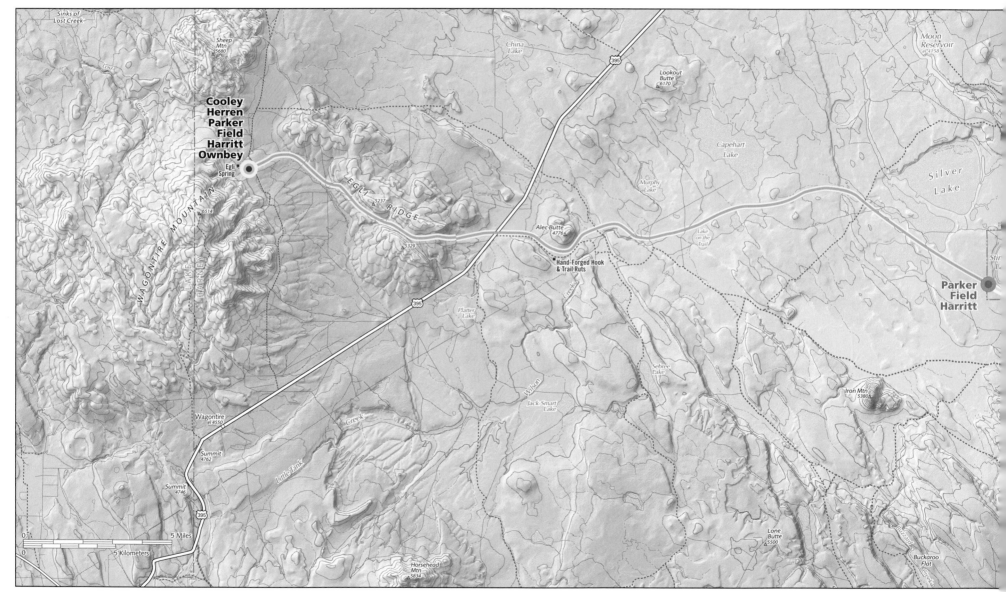

Cooley
Herren
Parker
Field
Harritt
Ownbey

Egli
Spring

Sinks of
Lost Creek

Sheep
Mtn
5680

WAGONTIRE MOUNTAIN

6514

LAKE HARNEY

EGLI RIDGE

5237

5329

China
Lake

395

Lookout
Butte
6170

Moon
Reservoir
el 4758

Capehart
Lake

Murphy
Lake

Silver
Lake

Alec Butte
4776

Lake
on the
Trail

■ Hand-Forged Hook
& Trail Ruts

Parker
Field
Harritt

Stir

395

Platter
Lake

Wilson

Creek

Sebree
Lake

Iron Mtn
5380

Jack Smart
Lake

Wagontire
el 4550

Summit
4762

Little Tank

Creek

Summit
4746

395

Lone
Butte
5500

Buzzard

0   5 Miles

0   5 Kilometers

Horsehead
Mtn
5834

Buckaroo
Flat

Creek

MAP 28 September 10, 1845

Cooley remained at Egli Spring. Field, Harritt, and Parker all traveled long distances to reach Egli Spring.

FIELD, HARRITT, AND PARKER ALL TRAVELED long distances to reach a campsite, probably at or near Egli Spring. Although the recorded distances varied (Field thirty miles, Harritt twenty-five miles, and Parker forty miles), the inaccuracies of the wagons' odometers or slightly different routes may have accounted for the discrepancies. In any case, all noted the difficult road. Parker's diary specifically mentions "Cursing and Swareing." Cooley "laid by" at Egli Spring.

Field comments on "hard, round nigger heads" encountered on that day's travel. While offensive today, the term in 1845 referred to black rock formations that were hard on wagons, oxen, and cattle.

PARKER: *went all day and all nite and struck A small Spring in the morning   Cursing and Swareing   105 wagons together   40*

COOLEY: *The Company laid by to day. Weather fine. Yesterday Mr. Wilborn started out to hunt water and lost his horse and when he got in to camp was almost ded. He was found in the road seting down resting and one of the men [torn corner] another company come there to nite from [torn corner] [written in bottom right margin "Spring"] gave him his horse and he got in to camp about*

Black rock formations the emigrants referred to as "nigger heads."

1 hour by Sun. Also about 100 head of cattle was let go off yesterday and was not got until the other company got in—several lost.

FIELD: *The ground about our encampment is encrusted with salt, which in some places may be scraped up with the hand in nearly pure state. Went about 30 miles today, over a road pretty well strewn with the hard, round nigger-heads frequently mentioned after leaving Ft. Hall, and camped after midnight at a spring where we found Owensby's company, which had arrived 24 hours before us. Their last camp was about seven miles this side of ours, and it was a dry one in the midst of wormwood barrens, so that they were nearly two days without water. We found about a hundred head of their stock between the two encampments, apparently nearly famished for water, and drove them on with us, but few of them giving out by the way although they looked miserable.*

HARRITT: *Made a late start; traveled a west course over a tolerable level road; very stony in places; found no grass or water for twenty-five miles; at one o'clock this morning we gradually descended a long slope, found a good spring affording an abundance of water and grass, with a few willows.*

THURSDAY, SEPTEMBER 11

Cooley traveled four miles and Parker traveled five to Lost Creek hollow. Field and Harritt rested at Egli Spring. According to Field's diary entry, Herren (with Ownbey) traveled to Lost Creek hollow.

COOLEY AND PARKER'S GROUPS LEFT EGLI SPRING about noon and traveled four or five miles around and between the ridges of Wagontire Mountain to the area known today as Lost Creek Spring or Lost Creek hollow on the northwest face of the mountain. Parker had no diary entries between September 11 and September 16. The words "water found" probably refer to the discovery of water several days later. Field describes Ownbey's group, which included Herren, as "in as much confusion as any set of fellows I have yet seen on the road." Harritt and Field, their companies exhausted, remained at Egli Spring on the eleventh.

Field's detailed diary entry for this date reflects the enormous disappointment in Meek's leadership as well as the emigrants' frustration at their inability to determine their location. Samuel Hancock's comment about the Lost Creek hollow camp and about Meek is also worth noting.

After journeying along in the most wretched way imaginable, both ourselves and stock destitute of water, we were about to despair

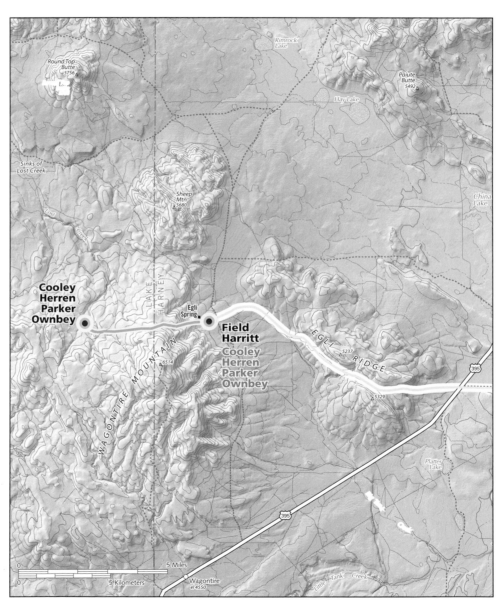

MAP 29 September 11, 1845

An aerial view of Wagontire Mountain. A section of the Lost Creek hollow campsite is on the right-hand side of the photograph.

when we came to two small springs, where we encamped, though there was very little grass; but we had water and were loth to leave it, not knowing where we could find more, if ever; our guide being interrogated as to our route in this direction, seemed entirely at a loss, and not disposed to commit himself, as to what we might expect in regard to water, the geography of the Country we were to encounter, or any other information we desired. Here there was decided uneasiness in camp, and we had thus far suffered so much under the guidance of this person, that it was probably well that he did not venture a prognostication as to our future, as it was now evident that he was totally unfamiliar with the country, as destitute of all things essential to an emigration party.

In commenting about Meek, Hancock additionally says:

A great deal of dissatisfaction was expressed in our company towards our guide, Mr. Meeks, and it was whispered that two gentlemen having about three hundred head of cattle between them had contracted privately with our guide to pilot the train into the Upper Willamette country for the extra sum of one hundred dollars, each, and the company to be kept ignorant of this arrangement, which it was thought had induced Mr. Meeks to depart from the route with which he was acquainted.

Anger with Meek would continue to build in the next few days.

PARKER: *went to Another Spring   5 laid heare 4 days and some five days   Codent find now water   frome 10 to 20 and 30 men out hunting water   Some Came in to Camp and Codent Speck   Water found*

COOLEY: *Weather fine today. Road some what broken and rockey. The corse about west. The company started after considerable confusion and 1 fite and come about 4 miles and camped at a spring. Plenty of grass and some wood and willow.   4 miles*

FIELD: *It being two o'clock this morning before we got to camp, we stuck to it the remainder of the day. Owensby's company left about noon for a camp six or seven miles ahead. His company are in as much confusion as any set of fellows I have yet seen on the road. Having lost confidence in Meek, many of them are trying to hunt a road for themselves. It seems there was a misunderstanding between us and Meek when we left Snake River respecting the route he intended taking. We understood him that on leaving the Malheur river he intended striking over to the John Day river and down it to the old road. When we found ourselves on the branches of the Deschutes river it rather surprised us, and as we had a report in camp of a few days before that he was going to pilot Owensby across the Cascade Mountains to the Willamette settlements, we supposed he was taking a straight shoot for them. It seems that he calls the Deschutes river the John Jay, which he says is the name by which it is known to the mountain traders, and the similarity in the sound of the two names made us mistake the one for the other. It was his intention to follow down Crooked river to the Deschutes and down it to the old road, but when he came to the marshy lake spoken of last Sunday, the company refused to follow him if he made the circuit necessary to get around it upon Crooked river again so he struck off in a westerly direction in order to get upon the main Deschutes River. He well knew that there was a scarcity of grass and water across here and so informed them, but it was nearer and they would have him go it, and now blame him for coming the route they obliged him to.*

HARRITT: *Laid by all day to rest our teams.*

FRIDAY, SEPTEMBER 12

One-third of Ownbey's company left Lost Creek hollow with their wagons, according to Field, and traveled toward the Sinks of Lost Creek. Cooley and Parker remained at Lost Creek hollow. Field and Harritt traveled six and five miles, respectively, to Lost Creek hollow.

- -

HARRITT AND FIELD BOTH FOLLOWED COOLEY'S and Parker's route to the Lost Creek hollow area. At this point, all of the diarists were together on the north face of Wagontire Mountain.

Cooley's diary and Samuel Hancock's reminiscence both comment on the arrival of other companies traveling the Meek Cutoff. Apparently, stragglers kept arriving daily and simply added to the water, food, and hygiene problems. Hancock says:

> Our company increased at these springs, and thirty wagons of our immediate company that had gone forward the day before, came back alarmed at the prospect before them, to find that other trains from the Atlantic side learning of the course we had taken, from the manager at Fort Boise, had followed us here having experienced the same difficulties that we had encountered, so that our company now numbered in wagons, one hundred and fifty. Parties left the camp in the direction we were to travel,

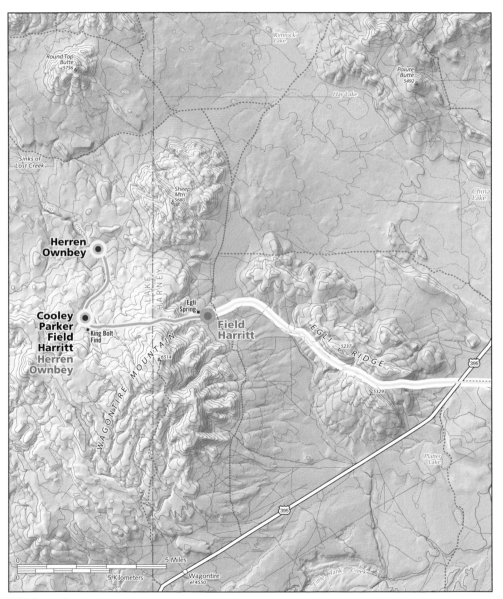

MAP 30 September 12, 1845

An aerial view of a small section of the Lost Creek hollow campsite.

in search of water and grass, and returned at night with the discouraging intelligence that none could be found; about ten o'clock at night our guide returned with the same information; the straggling grass around the encampment was soon consumed, though upon the hillsides among the rocks, frequent patches of bunch grass were found—enough to keep the animals alive.

The number of men on horseback constantly exploring the mountains in quest of water now numbered one hundred, fully impressed with the anxiety with which they were regarded by their fellow travelers; yet these explorations were continued seven days unsuccessfully; the excitement was intense, and famine seemed inevitable.

Field notes that about one-third of Ownbey's company moved out on the twelfth, likely to the Sinks of Lost Creek, which encompass a low-lying area where water from the creek has collected to form marshes or pools and then often vanishes by percolation or evaporation.

Cooley also notes the departure, made against the advice of Meek, who asked all the emigrants to remain at Wagontire Mountain while he searched for water. Respect for Meek's judgment continued to deteriorate.

When the expedition visited Lost Creek Hollow, we visited the spot where Del Hinshaw believed the Harritt group had camped. Our metal detectors found a large piece of iron, possibly a wagon king bolt, a vertical bolt connecting the body of a wagon with the fore axle. We marked the site and reburied it.

Several reminiscences discuss Meek's plight and the emigrants' problems at this time. W. W. Walter, an 1845 emigrant from Indiana who settled in the

Lost Creek hollow, Del Hinshaw's suggested Harritt campsite.

Lost Creek hollow. The Harritt campsite from a different perspective.

Touchet Valley near Prescott, Washington, wrote: "There were threats of hanging Meek, but it was thought he knew more than any one else about the Country, so it was not done."

Andrew Jackson McNamee, born March 5, 1848, and the son of emigrant Job McNamee, reminisced about a conversation with his father:

While the emigrants were camped in "Stinky Hollow" many of the oxen lay down and refused to get up, for when an ox is all in he quits. An ox will stay with it as long as he can, but when he finally gives up it is almost impossible to persuade him to get to his feet again. For three days, while the men were out hunting for the lost oxen, the party camped there, suffering from thirst. My father rode three horses till they were beat out looking for water. Upon his return to the camp he found three wagons that had been placed facing each other in the form of a triangle, their tongues raised and tied together at the top. The sullen and angry men of the party had put a rope around Steve Meek's neck and were about to hang him. My father, pointing his gun at the men, said, "The first man that pulls on that rope will be a dead man. Steve Meek is the only man who has ever been in this part of the country before. If you hang him, we are all dead men. If you give him a little time he may be able to recognize some land-mark here and find a way out." The men agreed to give Meek three days.

Elizabeth (Betsy) Bayley an emigrant, wrote to her sister in Ohio on September 20, 1849, describing the conditions at Lost Creek hollow.

Provisions were nearly exhausted; children were dying from want, exposure and mountain fever; sorrow and dismay were depicted on every countenance; several graves were made there. Over the dead body of his wife, one man swore to kill Meek on site.... We had men out in every direction, who traveled forty or fifty miles in search of water, but found none. Go back we could not, and we knew not what was before us.

PARKER: [No diary entry]

COOLEY: *Weather fine to day. A few of the wagons started to day and Riggs Company come in here. To day the pilot wanted the company to lay by until he took a hunt for water but some of them would not do so.*

FIELD: *Went about 6 miles camping upon another little spring which running a short distance sinks again. The ravine looks as though a smart branch ran through it at some seasons of the year. The hills around are covered with cedars; with the exception of the plain to the westward that appears to be the case with all the country to the north and west of us as far as the eye can reach, and that appears to be the Cascade mountains. Found two-thirds of Owensby's company still here, the remainder having gone on with the pilot and captain. A party of five men who left us last Tuesday morning to go back in search of the missing horses returned tonight bringing nine of them, which they had taken from a party of Indians near Crooked river. The Indians appeared loth to give them up but they charged upon them and took them, running the Indians off, who they say are a miserable set of wretches with no arms but bows and arrows.*

HARRITT: *Made a small move of five miles, and encamped on a small branch; found tolerable good grass and cedar timber in abundance.*

Possible wagon king bolt.

SATURDAY, SEPTEMBER 13

Harritt left Lost Creek hollow, traveled three miles, and then returned to his original camp. He probably traveled northwest up Lost Creek toward the "sinks." Field left the hollow, but four miles from camp he met Meek's wife, who said that no water had been found. He returned to Lost Creek hollow. Cooley and Parker remained at Lost Creek hollow. Ownbey, according to Field's September 14 diary entry, returned to the hollow.

COOLEY AND PARKER REMAINED AT LOST CREEK hollow. Field left the hollow but returned during the day, after meeting Meek's wife, who conveyed the ominous news that no water had been found.. Cooley writes, "Balance of the wagons started to day . . . but got word that they had not found no water so we returned to the spring again. The men that first started had to bring their oxen back to the spring for they had found no water." The "men that first started" probably refers to Ownbey's group that left on September 12 and returned on the thirteenth without their wagons, which had been left several miles from camp.

Written many years after the 1845 Lost Wagon Train disaster, W. W. Walter's reminiscence provides a good summation of the emigrant's situation: "We were all starving and sick, were out of Food,

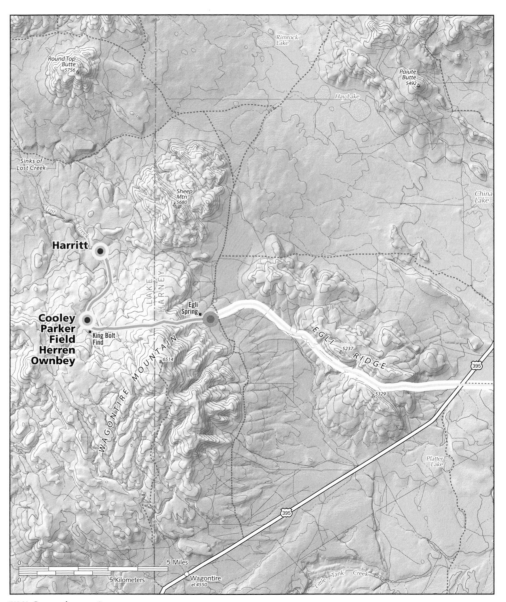

MAP 31 September 13, 1845

Aerial view of part of the Lost Creek hollow campground.

Lost Creek hollow.

eating emigrent [sic] cattle made many sick, the suffering was intense, we had no bread for weeks. If anything will try a person it is hardship such as we endured."

The emigrants were not only running out of food and water, but some sort of mountain fever was endemic in the camps. Clearly, the situation was becoming desperate.

When the expedition visited Lost Creek hollow we found a small creek, bordered by willows and juniper, running for two or three miles. The water flow was probably insufficient for 10 emigrant wagons, let alone 150 to 200 wagons and accompanying animals.

PARKER: [No diary entry]

COOLEY: *Weather fine to day. Balance of the wagons started to day and also Mr. Riggs company but got word that they had not found no water so we returned to the spring again. The men that first started had to bring their oxen back to the spring for they had found no water and took water back to the famileys to drink.*

FIELD: *Started this morning in expectation of a long drive across the plain before us, but when about four miles from camp met Meek's wife in company with a friend, returning with the news that they had found no water as yet and requesting all who were at the spring to remain*

there until he found a camp and returned or sent word back for them to come on. Nothing remained for us to do but drive back to the camp we had just left, where we found Teatherows company also, so if misery loves company here is enough of it, for this small camping spot is nearly eaten out by our own large stock of cattle, and to add to all this there are some in the company nearly out of provisions.

HARRITT: *Made a start, traveling three miles; met the man who had accompanied the pilot in search of water; found none; we returned to our old encampment, and stopped for the night.*

SUNDAY, SEPTEMBER 14

Harritt apparently "laid still." Cooley, Field, and Parker remained at Lost Creek hollow. Ownbey recovered his wagons and returned with them to the hollow. Solomon Tetherow and his company arrived at the hollow.

PARKER HAD NO DIARY ENTRY FOR THE FOUR-teenth, so he must have remained at Lost Creek hollow. Harritt simply noted that he also "laid still." Field, typically a more thorough diarist, noted that Ownbey's group, which departed Lost Creek hollow on the twelfth, returned on the thirteenth without their wagons. On the fourteenth, Ownbey and his group retrieved their wagons.

Meek, according to Cooley, spent the fourteenth searching for water. Field says that in the evening Meek returned and "said that from the tip of a mountain a short distance from here he had discovered a cut in the side of a mountain apparently 15 miles distant where from the bright green appearance of the willows and grass there could be no doubt of our finding water."

Many think the first mountain mentioned by Field is Glass Butte. In fact, our expedition climbed Glass Butte, the mountain north of Wagontire Mountain, with an elevation of 6,382 ft. It was a lengthy and difficult ascent. None of us believes that Meek or others of the party would have taken the time or expended the energy to make such a

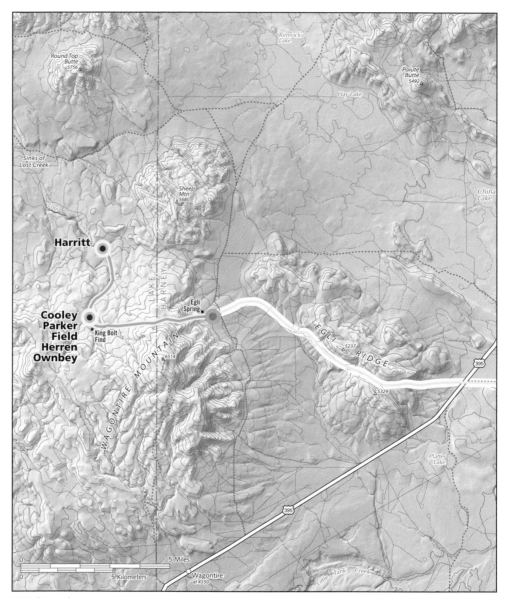

MAP 32 September 14, 1845

Looking north from Midnight Point to the GI Ranch. Buck Creek is in the haze in the upper middle of this photograph. Range fires created the smoky atmosphere; visibility was probably much better in 1845.

taxing climb. We then visited Midnight Point (5,112 ft. elevation), a ridge about four miles east of Glass Butte that offers an unobstructed view across the flats north to the springs of the GI Ranch. Midnight Point would have been a logical viewpoint for Meek and other Lost Creek hollow outriders. The vista includes Buck Creek, a few miles northeast of the GI Ranch site. Buck Creek flows out of what we believe is the second mountain identified in Field's diary. Facing north on our left was Glass Butte and slightly to the left, behind us, was Little Glass Butte. Round Top Butte was east of us. Seven miles to the south-east is the site of the Harritt camp in Lost Creek hollow. From Midnight Point it is possible, with bin-oculars and some imagination, to see some greenery at Buck Creek and even greenery around the springs of the GI Ranch, some fifteen miles north.

W. A. Goulder writes movingly about the emi-grants' desperation for water:

> Where all suffered so much, and where the greatest, or at least the most intense, suffer-ing fell upon the women and children of the party, it hardly seems right for me to speak of my own share in the common burdens. But I cannot refrain from here mentioning one little instance. In one of our dry camps, I had gone to bed in a tent after a day of most exhausting labor and unendurable thirst. In spite of this raging thirst, I soon fell asleep. I had a succes-sion of broken dreams, and at last thought that I was awake. I thought I heard a noise of rippling water, and while I listened, the welcome sound grew more and more distinct. I could no longer doubt. There was certainly a stream of water running past the rear of the tent. I jumped from

my couch, and ran out and around to the place where I had heard the rippling water. There I stopped, and stood quite still for a moment. I was really awake now, and the illusion was gone. I returned to my couch, carrying with me the same old thirst, now increased to tenfold intensity. I did not sleep any more that night, and so escaped the enjoyment of any further illusions.

Samuel Hancock is also worth quoting:

The feelings of our company towards the guide were of that unmistakable character to justify me in telling him his life was in danger; his reply was "I have known it for several days, but what can I do?   I have brought you here, and will take you off, if you will go." He then asked if our teams would follow: I told him that I thought a portion of this large train might be induced to follow, regarding, I must confess, the contingency of remaining here, or following this guide in whom none of us had the slightest confidence, as equally desperate. Many of us thought that at all events, the company had better separate as nothing was being accomplished by remaining together except greater distress; so we admonished the guide to secrete himself in one of our wagons and remain there; during this time inquiries were made after him by parties, who wished him to go with them in search of water, which was of no sort of use as the entire country had been explored; they were told that he had gone.

Incidentally, in his "career" as a mountain man, Meek learned how to survive in the western desert. In an article in the *Oregonian* of January 16, 1938, F. T. Humphrey quotes a pioneer from the 1845 train: "One of Meek's tricks, learned in the hard school of necessity, stood him in good stead on the 1845 crossing. Unable to get to water, Meek opened a vein in the neck of his mule and drank the blood, thus averting death from thirst. This incident was recounted . . . in a pioneer day address many years afterward . . . [by] . . . a member of the emigrant train."

PARKER: [No diary entry]

COOLEY: *Weather fine to day. Mr. Tethrow Companys got in here to day and the wagons xcept some 2 or 3 come back. To day still found no water and Mr. Meek is still hunting for water.   It is said that there is 4 companys back at the last encampment.*

FIELD: *Last evening the portion of Owensby's company which were out upon the plains returned with their cattle and water kegs, having left their wagons out upon the plain seven miles from here and no water had then been found within 30 miles of them. Today Meek ordered them to return to this place and sent an order for us to remain at this place until tomarrow morning, then to let 10 or 12 men accompany him with spades and dig for water at a place he thinks it can be found, in the dry bed of a creek. This evening Owensby returned with his wagons, teams, cattle and all, having enough of lying out upon the plain upon uncertainties. Meek came in after dark and said that from the tip of a mountain a short distance from here he had discovered a cut in the side of a mountain apparently 15 miles distant where from the bright green appearance of the willows and grass there could be no doubt of our finding water and requesting that some horsemen might accompany him to search the mountain sides still further; he thought there would be no danger in some wagons starting tomarrow.*

HARRITT: *Laid still all day, waiting for the return of the pilot, who returned late in the evening; found no water.*

MONDAY, SEPTEMBER 15

Harritt remained at or near the Sinks of Lost Creek. Cooley may have remained at Lost Creek hollow or may have moved to the sinks. Field remained at the hollow. Parker had no diary entry on the fifteenth, but must have departed for the springs of the GI Ranch. Parts of Ownbey's and Tetherow's companies departed Lost Creek hollow, traveling north for the possible water site discovered by Meek on the fourteenth.

COOLEY REMAINED AT EITHER LOST CREEK HOL-
low or near the Sinks of Lost Creek. Harritt laid by, although his brief entry notes that members of his company left camp searching for water.

Both Field and Cooley report that parts of Tetherow's and Ownbey's companies, accompanied by Meek, departed Lost Creek hollow in the afternoon and headed for "the spot spoken of yesterday, which lies northeasterly from here."

Parker made no diary entry on the fifteenth. On the seventeenth he traveled eleven miles to Camp Creek. If he left Lost Creek hollow on the sixteenth, he could not have traveled the twenty-five or thirty miles to the springs of the present-day GI Ranch and then left immediately and traveled eleven more miles to Camp Creek. Working backwards: Parker must have left Lost Creek hollow on the fif-

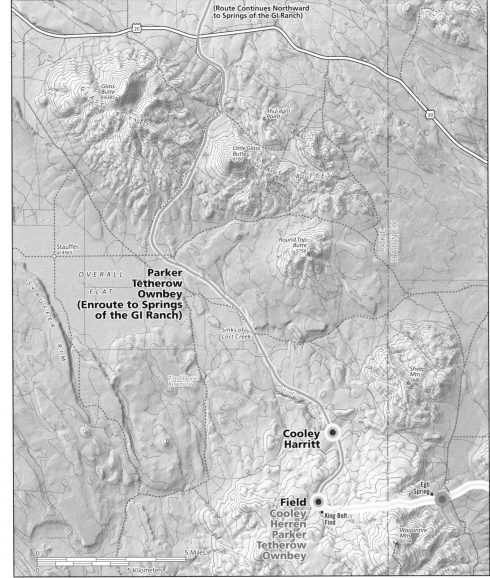

MAP 33 September 15, 1845

The route out of Lost Creek hollow and toward the gap between Glass Butte and Little Glass Butte. The Sinks of Lost Creek are on the tan flat on the left side of the photograph.

Emigrants probably traveled the route in the gap between Glass Butte and Little Glass Butte.

teenth and arrived at the GI Ranch springs on the sixteenth. (The GI Ranch, founded in the 1870s, is named after the first two initials of the original settlers' name. It is a half-million-acre cattle ranch now owned by the GI Ranch Corporation. It lies north and south of US Highway 20 some eighty-five miles east of Bend. The huge ranch includes properties in four counties.) The line of travel from Wagontire Mountain to the springs of the GI Ranch crosses GI property.

On the sixteenth, Field notes that Captain Riggs, accompanied by two other men, left camp on the fifteenth to confirm Meek's water discovery. Cooley's diary is unclear. It suggests that part of his company left Lost Creek hollow on the fifteenth with Tetherow.

There are numerous written descriptions of the emigrants' dire straits at Wagontire Mountain and of their trek north. Samuel Hancock writes:

About thirty wagons of our immediate company now commenced preparations for leaving, filling beef hides and everything that would contain water; we left the encampment about two o'clock in the day, feeling rather sad at leaving the others, with so much uncertainty of ever meeting them again. A good many of our company were sick, not only of heart, but body also, occasioned from scarcity of the proper kind of food; in fact we had been compelled to kill stock that we were desirous to save and bring to Oregon if it were possible to get there;

there being no game of any kind; however, these cattle would have died if we had not killed them as they were gradually sinking from the fatigue and privations they had had to endure.

W. W. Walter noted that the train

divided up . . . in small companies, but not far apart, untill [sic] we came to Stinking Hollow, where we all got together again, we could not find any water ahead, we we [sic] camped for over a week and sent our runners to find a camp ahead. There was a child born in that camp. We finally moved on, starting in the evening and traveling all night, untill some time the next day when we found water.

This account by Lucy Jane Hall, daughter of Captain Lawrence Hall, who apparently led one of the Meek companies, accurately represents the precarious situation of the emigrants as they left Lost Creek hollow and their excitement at reaching water:

We moved on till night. There was neither grass nor water to be found. All night the men sat by . . . camp fires listening for reports from those who had gone in search of water. If any was found a signal of three shots was to be fired in quick succession; if not three shots at intervals. At sunrise no sound had been heard. The train was soon moving on through sage brush and across dry creek beds which mocked our thirst. So we journeyed till noon, when . . . a shot, but not the three in quick succession, but at intervals; like a death knell they sounded. The men stood in groups talking over the situation, mothers, pale and haggard, sat in the wagons. . . . The party moved on. About night in quick succession shots were heard, which proclaimed that water had been found. All pushed forward with renewed energy. When in sight of the water the thirsty oxen broke into a run and rushed into the water and drank until they had to be driven out.

Hancock describes the elation felt by the emigrants as word of the discovery of water moved through the encampment. The excitement was contagious as they hurriedly departed Lost Creek.

It was now about five months since we took our departure from the Atlantic States and there was considerable sickness in our company. Notwithstanding this we traveled all the afternoon and night succeeding our departure from the rest of the emigration, and turned our cattle out to feed upon all they could get, and to obtain the dew that had fallen the night before; after this we started again and traveled all day; towards evening we gave our oxen a little of the water we had brought from the Springs, then continued traveling all night, allowing our animals to graze and avail themselves of the dew, as we did the day before and then started on the third day's drive from the Springs, first giving our teams a little water to enable them to proceed.

PARKER: [No diary entry.]

COOLEY: *Weather fine to day. Mr. Tetherow and a part of his company started to day late this evening and also some out of our company and arrived at camp onset day.*

FIELD: *This afternoon about three o'clock, 21 of Tetherow's together with 6 or 7 of Owensby's company made a start for the spot spoken of yesterday, which lies northeasterly from here, Meek accompanying them. A company of 8 or 10 wagons passed through the hollow we were encamped in, and started out into the plains by moonlight in the evening. They were a company we had never seen before and they said they were the last to leave the states for Oregon this year, starting some two or three weeks behind us. Their loose stock were nearly all working steers, they having enough apparently to change teams every day.*

HARRITT: *Despatched a company of men with their pack horses, loaded with water and provisions, in search of water.*

TUESDAY, SEPTEMBER 16

Harritt left his encampment, probably at the Sinks of Lost Creek, in the afternoon and traveled all night. He covered twenty-five miles, probably to Buck Creek. Cooley left Lost Creek hollow, but his diary and diary directions are very confused. He records twenty-four miles, so he probably traveled to the springs of the GI Ranch and arrived early in the morning on the seventeenth. Field left the hollow late in the afternoon and recorded twenty miles (although the distance is closer to thirty miles) to the springs of the GI Ranch—probably arriving early on the morning of the seventeenth. Parker arrived at the springs of the GI Ranch. Tetherow likely arrived at the springs of the GI Ranch on the sixteenth and left on the seventeenth. He camped near Cooley on the seventeenth.

- -

THE OUTRIDERS WHO LEFT HARRITT'S ENCAMPment at Lost Creek hollow on September 15 returned early in the morning on the sixteenth and reported finding water some twenty-five miles distant. Our expedition crossed some open uncultivated fields located three or four miles south of the GI Ranch springs. We believe the grasses of

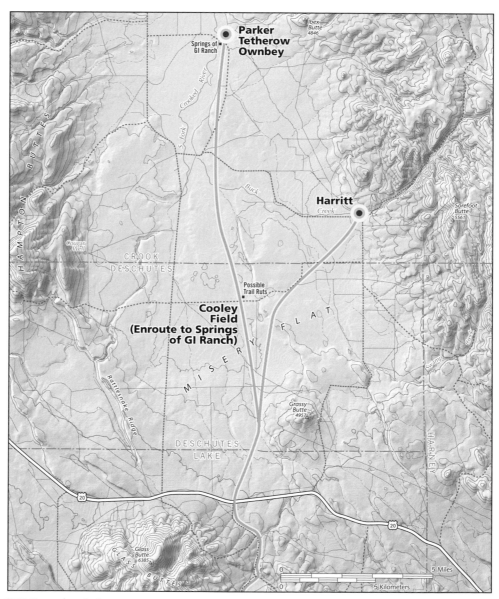

MAP 34 September 16, 1845

those fields, entirely different vegetation from the surrounding sagebrush, might have been visible from a spot such as Midnight Point. They would have suggested water to outriders who eventually located the springs.

We are reasonably certain that Harritt rested at Buck Creek since his diary description seems to match the actual site: "At daybreak we reached the place of encampment at a small mountain stream, winding its way through a level valley; found no wood except sage, which grew in abundance near its margin."

Parker's group traveled all night, and reached the springs of the GI Ranch around sunrise on September 16. He reports traveling thirty miles.

Field notes that Riggs and the two men accompanying him returned to Lost Creek hollow on the morning of the sixteenth confirming Meek's discovery of water and grass: "We made preparation for starting immediately, but could not get ready until late in the afternoon, as our cattle were so scattered. We had a clear, full moon to light us on our toilsome way, which lay across a mountain to the northward, and after traveling about 20 miles we reached the long sought spot at daybreak."

Cooley's diary entry for September 16 is again confusing and full of locational discrepancies. His route, as he describes it, would have placed his September 17 campsite somewhere near the town of Hampton Butte, but there is no surface water within miles of that tiny community. In fact, Cooley's com-

Grassy area three to four miles south of the springs of the GI Ranch.

Buck Creek flowing out of the hills onto the desert floor.

pany apparently came together several miles north of Lost Creek hollow on the morning of the sixteenth and probably traveled north to Buck Creek and the springs of the GI Ranch on the latter part of the sixteenth and the morning of the seventeenth. Cooley's diary notes that his company camped close to Tetherow's company on the evening of the seventeenth.

Historians and local history buffs have long argued about the location of the emigrant route from Lost Creek hollow to the springs of the GI Ranch. Del Hinshaw believed they traveled west around Glass Butte. Others think the emigrants went east around Little Glass Butte, probably incorrectly referred to as "Round Butte" by annotators. Either route would be out of the way for people desperately seeking water. While we will probably never know conclusively, the gap between Glass Butte and Little Glass Butte seems the most likely path of travel, although we found no definitive trail ruts. It is the shortest, quickest route to Buck Creek and the springs of the GI Ranch.

Buck Creek, located a few miles southeast of the GI Ranch, may well have been the first stop for many of the emigrants after leaving Lost Creek hollow. It was, after all, a source of water and in their desperation emigrants who saw the green grass around Buck Creek may have rested there before going several miles farther to the springs of the GI Ranch.

It appears that Samuel Hancock traveled with a group that departed Lost Creek hollow on the sixteenth and arrived at the springs on the seventeenth. He says:

Misery Flat just north of Glass Butte. From the helicopter, we observed some faint tracks appearing to come from the gap between Glass Butte and Little Glass Butte. Could they be from the 1845 train?

Just before sunset . . . we heard a number of shots fired in the direction we were going and afterwards the firing was renewed much nearer to us; looking forward we discovered a man coming at full speed on horseback—our guide had found water!

It is impossible to describe the joy with which this news was received; some were so overcome that they could not give utterance to their feelings of joy, while tears of gratitude streamed down their cheeks, others gave vent to their delight in loud exultations; the women and children clapping their hands and giving other demonstrations that they too were enraptured by the announcement of plenty of water. In fact the poor animals seemed to have an appreciation of it too for it is said in scarcity an animal can smell food or water at a great distance; at any rate they traveled along apparently more cheerfully. At the time we received information of our approach to water, we could not have been more than five miles distant from a tributary of the De Shutes River, which we reached very hurriedly as might be imagined and were once again greeted with the sight of plenty of water and grass.

The gap south of Glass Butte.

Little Glass Butte from the summit of Glass Butte. The train likely traveled through the gap.

Emigrant Elizabeth Bayley also describes reaching water: "The wearied animals . . . quickened their pace till it was almost a trot; they smelled water. Finally the men had to unhitch the oxen, when there was a general stampede to the water. The animals would rush in all over,—leaving only their heads out."

PARKER: *left at 3 p m oclock traveled all nite   Come to water at Sunrise   30   Missis But now betor [Mrs. Butts no better]   198 wagons in Company   2,299 loose Cattle   oxen 811 head   all thes Cattle to git water and 1051 Gotes also consume A heap of water*

COOLEY: *Weather fine to day. All of our wagons that had started out the other day got in to day. News come that thare was water and this evening we started and got to a branch onset morning at sun rise. Traveled down the hollow out at the Mouth which is about 2 miles and along the way wee first started for about 3 miles further. The corse this far is about South west. Then wee turned to the rite and traveled about a North corse for about 19 miles and camped on a branch. Plenty of grass and some willow and plenty of sage here. For 5 miles the road is good; then rocky and some what broken for about 15 miles then good and level to the branch.   24 miles*

FIELD: *Capt. Riggs accompanied by the two Wilcoxes started yesterday to search for water at a place they had seen the day before, and which the description given by Meek of the spot he expected to find water at, applied to precisely. They returned this morning reporting it the same with plenty of water and grass. We made preparation for starting immediately, but could not get ready until late in the afternoon, as our cattle were so scattered. We had a clear, full moon to light us on our toilsome way, which lay across a mountain to the northward, and after traveling about 20 miles we reached the long sought spot at daybreak.*

HARRITT: *The hunters returned this morning at nine o'clock; found water; in a few minutes the company were in parade for their oxen made a general collection of stock; between four o'clock and sundown about eighty wagons left the branch for the next encampment; traveled all night; at daybreak we reached the place of encampment at a small mountain stream, winding its way through a level valley; found no wood except sage, which grew in abundance near its margin; having come twenty-five miles we stopped to take some refreshments and rest our teams.*

WEDNESDAY, SEPTEMBER 17

From this date forward, until rejoining several weeks later at Sagebrush Springs near Madras, Oregon, the train separated into two sections. Cooley, Herren, Tetherow, and others traveled west along the southern edge of the Maury Mountains. The remaining emigrants traveled north down the Crooked River. *Northern Route*: Parker left the springs of the GI Ranch on the morning of the seventeenth and traveled eleven miles, probably to Sand Hollow. Field remained at the springs all day. Harritt traveled six miles from Buck Creek to the springs. *Western Route*: Cooley, after resting until noon, traveled six miles, probably to the Clover Creek area. Tetherow's company traveled near or with the Cooley group.

- -

HARRITT TRAVELED SIX MILES, ABOUT THE DISTANCE from Buck Creek to the springs of the GI Ranch. His diary refers to a campsite on "a delightful stream running to the northwest, affording an abundance of fine grass—no wood." That phrase describes the springs that simply rise out of the high desert with neither willows nor other bushy vegetation to mark their appearance. The springs are the

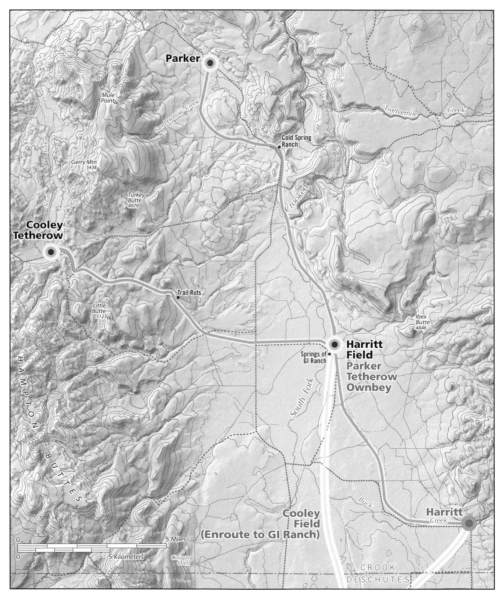

MAP 35 September 17, 1845

An aerial view of the springs of the GI Ranch.

The springs of the GI Ranch.

The springs of the GI Ranch.

headwaters of the Crooked River. The river flows in a northwesterly direction from the springs.

Parker had reached the springs of the GI Ranch on the sixteenth. After resting there for the remainder of the day, he departed on the morning of the seventeenth and traveled eleven miles. While Del Hinshaw shows Parker's route of travel in a generally westward direction to a campsite on Clover Creek, a close reading of the map plus well-defined ruts, cut stumps, and drag logs indicate that Parker, and at least some of the other emigrants, traveled to Sand Hollow. Photo descriptions of that eleven-mile journey are documented on September 18 when Harritt and Field followed Parker's trail.

Field arrived at the springs on the morning of the seventeenth and must have stayed all day. His diary states that he "lay by today."

Field's diary suggests that three companies were together at the springs. To Del Hinshaw, who annotated Field's diary, this indicates Tetherow had departed earlier. This suggestion is confirmed by Cooley's diary of the seventeenth, which states that Tetherow camped near Cooley that evening. Clark

and Tiller in *Terrible Trail* note that Tetherow's party now included the Herren group. (Incidentally, while most of the diaries were annotated, I learned that the annotators' comments were often in error. I suspect some of the annotators were looking at a map on a desk and had probably never tried to trace the trail.)

Cooley's diary states that he arrived at the springs of the GI Ranch about sunrise on September 17 and, after resting until noon, traveled

Ruts on the trail between the springs of the GI Ranch and Clover Creek. The trail parallels or is identical to the old Roberts-to-Fife freight road. Both Steve Lent and Del Hinshaw are certain the freight road followed the Meek Trail. Clearly, the freight road has been used by modern vehicles.

six miles farther before camping. An article in the *Oregonian* of April 27, 1919, noted that "Mrs. Millican [wife of George Millican, who homesteaded Hope Ridge between Bend and Burns off Highway 20] says that Straub Price of Prineville, who had a ranch at Hampton Butte, informed her that parties once found an ox yoke near the butte that had Sol Tetherow's name carved on it." Cooley's and Tetherow's exact campsite is difficult to determine. Clover Creek is some eight or nine miles from the springs of the GI Ranch. It is possible that a faulty odometer might have caused the discrepancy.

Like Field, Harritt rested all day at the springs.

As mentioned earlier, the train, for unknown reasons, split into two sections within a mile or two north of the GI Ranch springs. Diarists Field, Har-

Cooley and Tetherow's 1845 route winding through the sagebrush toward Clover Creek.

Clover Creek area.

An aerial view of the probable Clover Creek campsite. The springs of the GI Ranch are behind the hills in the center of the photo.

ritt, and Parker traveled north while Cooley and Tetherow went west. Many days later, these two sections reunited just south of Madras, Oregon.

On the evening of September 17, Harritt and Field were resting at the springs of the GI Ranch. Parker was a day ahead at Sand Hollow, and Cooley, with Tetherow's party nearby, probably camped at Clover Creek.

The expedition briefly explored Clover Creek, a logical campsite and definitely the campsite according to Del Hinshaw. About a mile south of Clover Creek we found two springs and an attractive open field. This would have been a satisfactory camping spot as well. There is a full flowing spring at this site.

Northern Route

PARKER: *went to A Creek* II

FIELD: *We are now nearer or as near the spring from which we made the 30 mile stretch on the 10th inst. as at the camp after we had made it, and this too after lying in vexatious suspense, camped in a little, narrow, barren, rockey hollow among the mountains, with the dry plain some 40 or 50 miles in extent before us, with the delightful anticipation that we would be obliged to cross it before reaching water. Nor was this all; more than one family have shaken the last flour from their sack, and others could calculate to a certainty the day they would do likewise. Lay by today, wishing to get a smaller company if possible, three large ones being mixed together.*

HARRITT: *After taking some refreshments we yoked our teams, at two o'clock P.M., traveled six miles and encamped on Sandy—a delightful stream running to the northwest, affording an abundance of fine grass—no wood.*

Western Route

COOLEY: *This morning wee camped about sun rise and about 12 o'clock started again and in about 6 miles struck a spring creek and camped near the head. Plenty of grass, some sage, no willow. Mr. Tetherow started this morning and camped just below us. Weather fine. 6 miles*

THURSDAY, SEPTEMBER 18

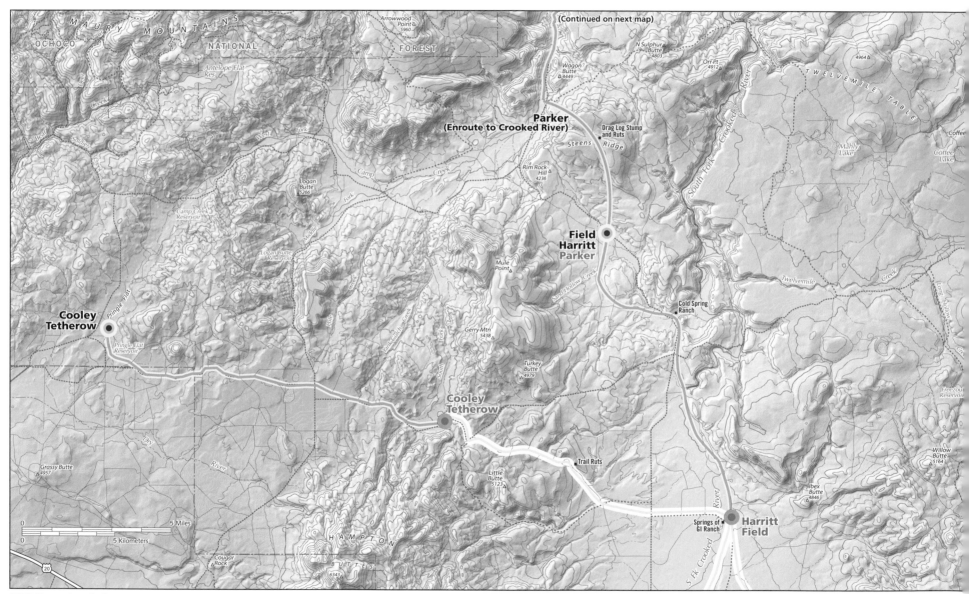

MAP 36 September 18, 1845

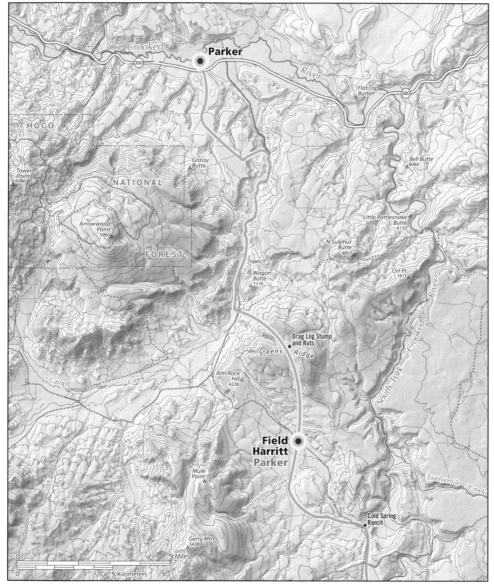

MAP 37 September 18, 1845

Northern Route: Parker traveled fifteen miles to the Crooked River. Field traveled with Harritt to Sand Hollow. *Western Route*: Cooley and Tetherow traveled fifteen miles, most likely to Pringle Flat.

- -

STEVE LENT OFTEN VISITS WITH RANCHERS IN the area and has led many tours retracing this section of the Meek Trail. He states that local historical lore, as well as topography, strongly suggests that the wagons reached Sand Hollow or Sand Hollow Creek. Today it is just a barren, sagebrush covered flat.

Northern Route

Harritt left the springs of the GI Ranch and apparently traveled some twelve miles northwest to Sand Hollow. Field traveled with Harritt. Their odometers recorded essentially the same mileage. Field describes his campsite "Traveled about 11 miles in a northwesterly direction, striking a smart sized creek running in the same direction and camping upon it. This creek has no brush upon its banks, which was the reason for its being overlooked when they searched the country for water."

Parker traveled fifteen miles, moving north from Sand Hollow to and down Steens Ridge, then down Cemetery Ridge to the south fork of the Crooked River.

Sand Hollow.

Cut stumps and drag logs near the top and down the slope of Steens Ridge clearly mark the emigrants' trail. The steep ridge above Camp Creek shows the remains of wagon ruts descending several hundred feet to the creek bottom. Descending upper sections of the ridge required ropes and drag logs tied to the back of the wagons to slow the descent.

Western Route

On the western route, Cooley traveled fifteen miles, probably down Clover Creek and then west to Pringle Flat.

Pringle Flat is a lovely prairie with year-round water and a huge open field inviting good camping. However, we found no visible signs of the emigrants' visits. (Incidentally, Kathleen Eloise Rockwell, better known as "Klondike Kate," the famous dancer and vaudeville actress of the Klondike Gold Rush, left the far north in 1902 and eventually moved near

The trail off Steens Ridge.

A drag log was cut from this stump, adjacent to the trail near the top of Steens Ridge.

Examining the trail coming off the top of Steens Ridge. Note the break in the rimrock in the upper center of the photo. This is the only spot where the wagons could come through the rimrock.

Pringle Flat. I met her at the Multnomah Hotel in Portland when she was near the end of her life. Her "charms" were long gone.)

Northern Route

PARKER: *over hills and Rock all day   Come down A Steep hill   got water   15*

FIELD: *Traveled about 11 miles in a northwesterly direction, striking a smart sized creek running in the same direction and camping upon it. This creek has no brush upon its banks, which was the reason for its being overlooked when they searched the country for water. It is evident that Meek's knowledge of the country has rather failed him here, since it is actually a shorter drive from* the spring we left on the 10th inst. to the head of the branch we camped upon yesterday than it is from the 10th to the 11th, and apparently a better road. Had we taken that road we would be advanced now at least 80 miles on our journey, besides being saved the trying suspense of remaining in a miserable encampment several days, with no prospect of water ahead for 40 or 50 miles.

HARRITT: *Three miles down we crossed over the west side and after a travel of twelve miles we encamped at a good spring; found good grass, and some cedar timber.*

Western Route

COOLEY: *Weather fine to day. Road tolerable good. Come down the creek North west about 3 miles and crossed it* and in about 11 miles further struck a hollow and come down about 1 mile further and camped at a spring. Plenty of grass and some wood on the bluff here.   15 miles

Aerial view of Pringle Flat.

Pringle Flat.

A sagging dance hall at Pringle Flat. Local inhabitants have said that in the early part of the twentieth century, people came from as far as seventy miles to socialize and dance the night away.

Expedition members exploring the trace off Steens Ridge.

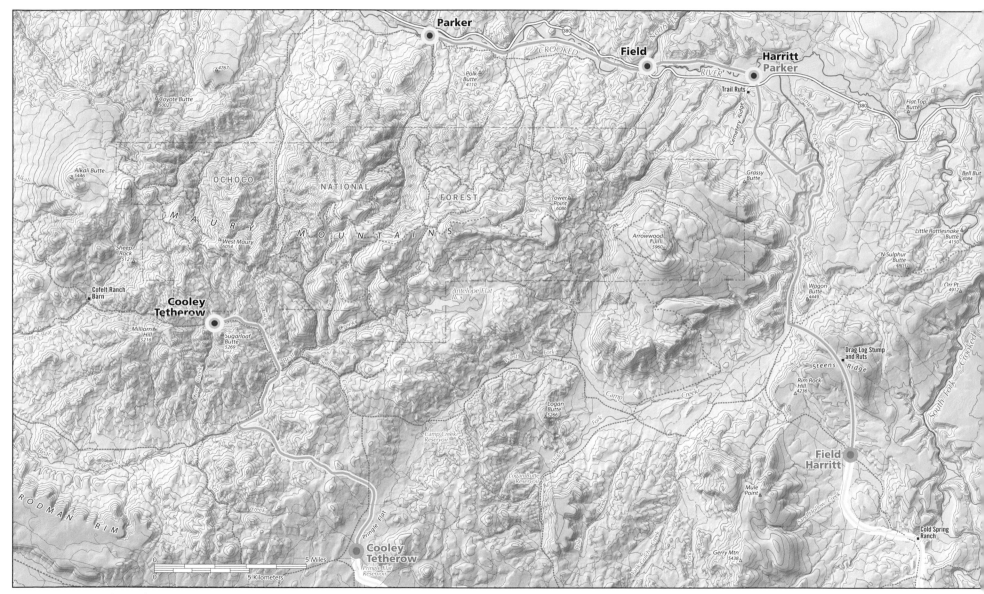

MAP 38 September 19, 1845

Trail coming down from Cemetery Ridge. Some years ago, the ranch owner's workman, unfortunately, made a diagonal cut across the trail.

1960 photograph of ruts off Cemetery Ridge.

Northern Route: Parker traveled seven miles down the Crooked River. Field traveled about twenty miles to and down the river. Harritt traveled twelve miles to the river. *Western Route:* Cooley traveled ten miles to or near Cow Creek.

- -

PARKER, NOW LEADING THE NORTHERN GROUP, traveled down the Crooked River drainage. Field and Harritt, traveling in Parker's footsteps, crossed the eastern end of the Maury Mountains. They then descended Cemetery Ridge to the Crooked River and went along the river. The parties had now suf-ficient water and grass to complete the trip to The Dalles. Moreover, at this point they had a good idea of their location. Although the emigrants contin-ued to suffer and to die, our expedition ceased fol-lowing the northern group's trail. We believe that their further suffering resulted primarily from their desperate journey from Vale to the springs of the GI Ranch when they were lost in the high desert and trackless wasteland that characterize parts of eastern Oregon.

Cooley, taking the western route, indicates that his company traveled ten miles. While his diary description is impossible to decipher, we believe that he traveled to Bear Creek, up Ferguson Creek, and camped in the Cow Creek area. Alonzo Gesner, a three-year-old child accompanying his parents on the 1845 train, later drew his suggested route of that part of the Meek Trail on an 1876 township survey map reproduced on page 131. Perhaps Gesner knew where the tracks were through family discussions. We found no evidence to support or disagree with his route but believe the most likely route is the one marked on our map.

Cooley's words, "Tetherow just below on the creek." is definitive evidence that Tetherow and Cooley were together at that point.

While our expedition found no evidence of the trail, Bill McCormack, owner of the McCormack Ranch headquartered at the confluence of Bear and Ferguson Creeks, and Steve Lent, our highly

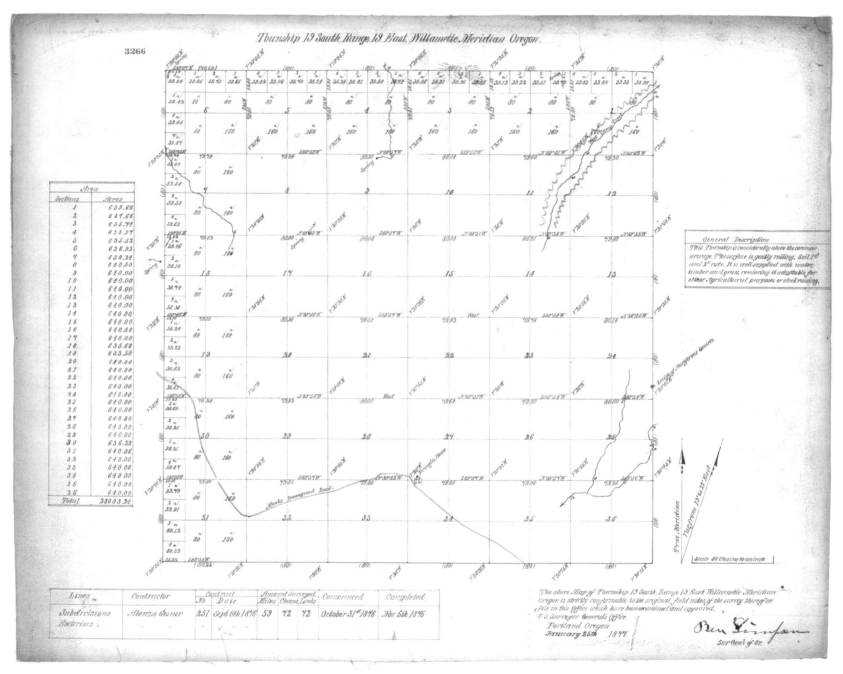

Alonzo Gesner's original survey of Township 19 South, Range 19 East, surveyed in 1876.

knowledgeable expedition member, are both convinced that the emigrants traveled up Ferguson Creek, north around the base of Houston Butte, then Sugarloaf Butte. They probably camped on Cow Creek or a tributary, Calf Creek, located a mile or so west of Cow Creek. The general area has abundant water and grass.

Northern Route

PARKER: *down the Creek some times in and sometimes out   7*

FIELD: *Went about 20 miles, road tolerably rough much of the way, camping upon a stream in a deep, narrow glen resembling the Malheur much in character and which we believe to be Lohum's fork of the Deschutes or Falls river.*

HARRITT: *Made an advance of twelve miles and encamped again on the Sandy, found grass and fine small willows.*

Western Route

COOLEY: *Road tolerable good today. Weather fine. Come down the branch about 2 mile and turned to the left up the hill and in about 5 mile struck the same creek wee crossed yesterday and traveled down it about 3 mile and camped. Plenty of grass and some willow. Tetherow just below on the creek. The corse to the creek is about North west then down the creek this far about west to north west. Some good to see us.   10 miles*

Aerial view of Ferguson Creek where it intersects with the McCormack Ranch. We believe the Cooley and Tetherow parties traveled up this creek bed.

The Cow Creek area.

Aerial view of probable Cow Creek campground.

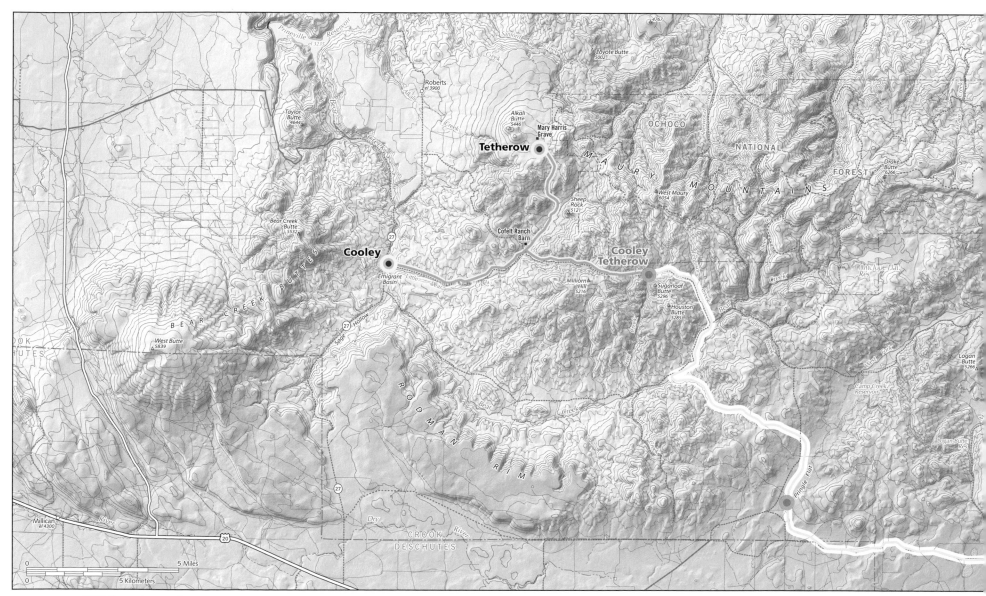

MAP 39 September 20, 1845

Cooley traveled from Cow Creek to the present day site of the Coffelt barn and then down Little Bear Creek to the junction with Bear Creek. Tetherow apparently made a right turn at the Coffelt barn site and camped in an open space just south of Alkali Butte.

HINSHAW AND THE MEMBERS OF THE MEEK Research Expedition believe that September 20 might have been an extremely important day in the emigrants' trek across eastern Oregon. It could have marked the date of the Blue Bucket gold discovery. Cooley's diary indicates he traveled twelve miles down a creek and that he camped on that creek. We suspect that Cooley and Tetherow traveled north around Milliorn Hill to the present-day Coffelt barn on Little Bear Creek. There they separated and Cooley traveled down Little Bear Creek. From his mileage, Cooley probably camped at or near the junction of Little Bear Creek with Bear Creek. In fact, the flat area at the junction is known locally as Emigrant Basin.

Today, traveling down Little Bear Creek in a wagon would be extremely difficult if not impossible. The creek flows through deeply eroded areas, some many feet deep. The rutted terrain is the result of overgrazing, which destroys vegetation that retains water. While fire destroys the canopies allowing regrowth of sagebrush, new juniper, bushes, and a

Emigrant Basin.

Eroded trail ruts in the Cow and Calf Creek area. This trail has likely been used by many others.

An aerial view looking up the Little Bear Creek watershed toward Alkali Butte on the left. Sheep Rock is in the middle of the photograph.

The Coffelt barn.

Sheep Rock in the distance.

variety of other plants, humans, over the centuries, have tried to minimize the natural cycle of brush-fires. The result is that relatively flat stream beds and surrounding areas are often deeply eroded, with the stream a tiny rivulet fifteen or twenty feet below the level of the land. Little Bear Creek is a perfect example. The pioneers likely found easy travel on a gently sloping terrain.

We are confident that Tetherow ascended the Little Bear Creek drainage and camped on the flats immediately south of Alkali Butte.

The expedition found ruts and a trail, probably traveled by Cooley and Tetherow in 1845 and used by others later, which ascends Milliorn Hill and then descends to the Coffelt barn on Little Bear Creek. The barn and ranch are currently owned by Wendy Rubbert. For years, the property was known as the Coffelt Ranch and, later, as the Nye Ranch.

Expedition member Steve Lent spent considerable time reviewing the Cooley diary and his comments are of interest:

I believe that Cooley's group of wagons went a different route than the others of the Tetherow group after reaching Little Bear Creek. On reaching the site of the Coffelt barn, instead of going up Little Bear Creek past Sheep Rock, he turned down Little Bear Creek to Bear Creek and then again hit the Tetherow group trail near the Dunham Ranch. He [Cooley] mentions returning to the same creek that they had been on a few days earlier and following it. He also does not mention being in the company of other wagons.

There are a number of Herrens involved in the story. John Daniel Herren was the diarist on the Meek Cutoff. His son, W. J. Herren, was the purported discoverer of the Blue Bucket nuggets. Daniel Herren, the nephew of John D. Herren, was also a Meek Cutoff emigrant. W. J. Herren's son, W. H. Herren, sent a letter to the *Oregonian* of March 7, 1922 which will be of interest to the reader. From the Coffelt barn, the vista up Little Bear Creek matches the description in this letter. He wrote: "Several of the young men that had saddled horses scouted the country over

Sheep Rock.

Probable Tetherow trail into the September 20 campsite on the flat south of Alkali Butte.

and finally found a ridge that led to the summit of the mountain. They concluded that if they could once get their outfits up on to this ridge they could make it over the mountains. By hitching ten and sometimes 12 yoke of oxen at a time to a wagon they finally succeeded in getting them up onto the divide."

From the Coffelt barn our expedition traveled up the long grade past Sheep Rock to an open flat just below Alkali Butte. The grade would probably require double or triple teaming of oxen to pull the wagons. On the flat we found at least one and perhaps two graves. The trail runs to the left of the graves, perhaps fifty to a hundred feet away. The flat area is now covered with sagebrush but we could easily imagine a dry campsite. The name associated with the largest grave is Mary E. Harris, of whom little is known. In an article in the March 26, 1916, *Oregonian,* two Baker, Oregon, prospectors, J. W.

Buckley and K. C. Harpan, describe finding "a rude head stone bearing the inscription 'Mary E. Harris—1849.'" Del Hinshaw, in a document in the possession of the author, notes that Mary E. Harris was listed in an 1845 death list by Hiram Smith, an 1845 emigrant.

As noted above, the campsite is adjacent to Alkali Butte, whose location is occasionally mentioned in emigrant reminiscences.

W. H. Herren's letter to the *Oregonian* continues:

When they reached the summit of the mountains they camped on a meadow, and while there some Warm Spring Indians came to their camp. One of the Indians could speak a little English. He told them that if some of them would go with him to a high ridge near by they could see down into the Deschutes and

Crooked river valleys. He showed them some buttes that lay south of present day Prineville and said that they would find water there, but no water between there and the Deschutes. He also showed them what is now called pilot Butte and told them if they would steer straight for that butte they would find a place in the bend of the river where a man could cross it on a horse, and for them to cross the Deschutes there and keep down the west side through by way of the Metolius and Tygh valley and that they would eventually reach The Dalles.

W. H. Herren associates the Blue Bucket gold discovery with this site. He continues:

There was no water on the divide so they had to make a dry camp. The captain of the company

[Tetherow] told all of the young people who had saddle horses to take buckets and go hunt for water. My father, who was then 23 years old, and his sister, who afterwards became the wife of William Wallace, took their old blue wooden buckets and started out to find water.

They finally found a dry creek bed which they followed until they found a place where a little water was seeping through the gravel, and while my father was digging for water his sister saw something bright and picked it up.

The account given me states that they found two good sized lumps or nuggets, and that there were many fine particles in the gravel. He was quite sure that it was gold at the time, and when he arrived at camp he showed it to some of the older men, who told him that if it was gold it would be mallable. So one of them took a hammer and hammered both pieces out flat into a saucer-shaped disc.

The *Oregonian* of July 21, 1908, contained the obituary of Daniel Herren, the nephew of John D. Herren:

It was during the journey from Missouri to Oregon in 1845, when the emigrant train had lost its way and was wandering among the head waters of the Malheur River, that Dan Herren picked up the pieces of yellow metal that afterward gave rise to all the golden stories of the "Blue Bucket Mines." He himself later searched for

Mary Harris grave.

An aerial view of the graves on Alkali Butte.

Aerial view from Alkali Butte looking toward the Cascade Range.

the spot, and hundreds of others have devoted much time to the quest; but the location has never again been discovered.

Cooley had separated from Tetherow on the morning of the twentieth, so he was not there to record such an event, if it actually occurred. There are no known diaries from Tetherow's party. The expedition members who visited the Alkali Butte area and spent the better part of two days searching there believe the discovery might have occurred on the evening of September 20 or possibly on the evening of the nineteenth near Cow Creek. This possibility was of great interest to all of us during our day-by-day search for visual evidence of the route

and of campsites. Please refer to the subheading "Gold" on page 23 and following pages for a more complete discussion of the purported discovery.

In fact, Del Hinshaw believed the gold discovery occurred on September 20 near the campsite on Alkali Creek, a stream running northwest just north of the campsite and south of Alkali Butte. He thought that a cave in or landslide may have covered the area of discovery. Since the expedition found a likely campsite with water on Cow Creek, but a totally dry campsite on Alkali Butte, and since so many commentators stressed the dry campsite at the time of the discovery, we spent extra time searching the Alkali Butte area. Much to our disappointment, we found nothing!

COOLEY: *Badd road to day. Weather fine. Traveled down the creek to day and generally in the bottoms of it some scattering seder and pine timber on the hills. They is plenty of grass and willow to camp any whare on the creek. Camped on the creek. Plenty of grass and wood here.   12 miles*

SUNDAY, SEPTEMBER 21

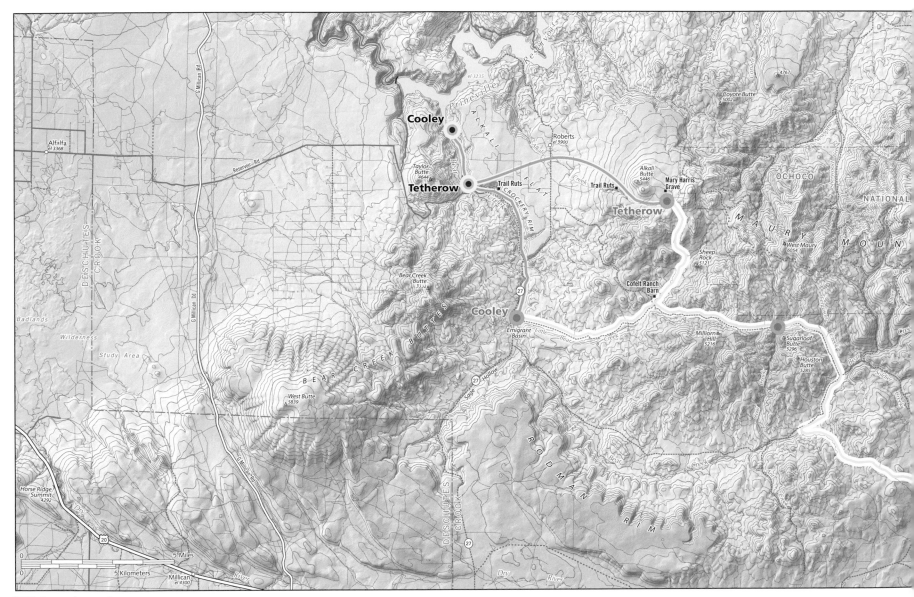

MAP 40 September 21, 1845

The trail down Alkali Butte.

Cooley traveled twelve miles northwest down Bear Creek.

- -

COOLEY PROBABLY CAMPED WELL BEYOND WHAT is cited on maps as the Dunham Ranch west of Alkali Flat. In fact, twelve miles from Emigrant Basin would place Cooley's September 21 campsite underwater in the Prineville Reservoir, constructed in 1964. In any case, it was impossible for the expedition to interpret Cooley's diary on this date with any degree of confidence.

Tetherow came west down Alkali Creek, then probably dropped over and down Crockery Rim and camped somewhere near the Dunham Ranch. The expedition members walked down Alkali Creek on a rutted trail probably used by Tetherow.

Eddie Campbell, a resident of Prineville, wrote this author on May 21, 1976, noting that some sixty years earlier, when he was a young man, he found "quite sizable ruts" across Alkali Flat west of Alkali Butte: "I told my dad about it and he said, 'You've found the old Emigrant trail.' The pioneers apparently crossed the flat near what is now known as

An aerial view of Crockery Rim.

Roberts. From Roberts—across latter day homesteads... mostly down through the McElroy Ranch ... and ... over the rim to the Dunham Ranch ... Mr. McElroy showed me broken china ware and part of a primitive sewing machine where a wagon tipped over. Heartbreak for the pioneer wife."

The ranch at the top of the rim is now owned by Bill Armstrong. The old Dunham Ranch is now owned by Ron Miller.

We then drove down Bear Creek road and hiked up to Crockery Rim. We found two or three drag logs, but no remnants of the broken ceramics or bottles that early searchers found. The steepness of the grade, however, and the six-hundred-foot drop in elevation from the rim left us in awe of the wagons and emigrants that traversed such an extremely sharp descent. The elevation at the Crockery Rim ridge is 3,865 feet. On the valley floor at the Dun-

Looking up Crockery Rim.

Close-up of Crockery Rim.

ham Ranch the elevation is 3,286 feet. On top of the rimrock is a cut that appears to be the only possible place the emigrants and their wagons could have come down. Descending the slope, we found a trace where the emigrants may have moved rocks to facilitate the descent.

In a letter to Mrs. J. E. Meyers of Prineville in the 1920s, W. H. Herren wrote: "They stated that they had a hard time gettin[g] down the western slope of the mountains, and that . . . they were compelled to let their wagons down with ropes on account of the steep places."

COOLEY: *Still bad road. Weather fine. Traveled down the creek to day and have crossed it several times to day and have camped on it. Plenty of grass and willow here and all along on the creek still seder and pine on the hills. West.   12 miles*

MONDAY, SEPTEMBER 22

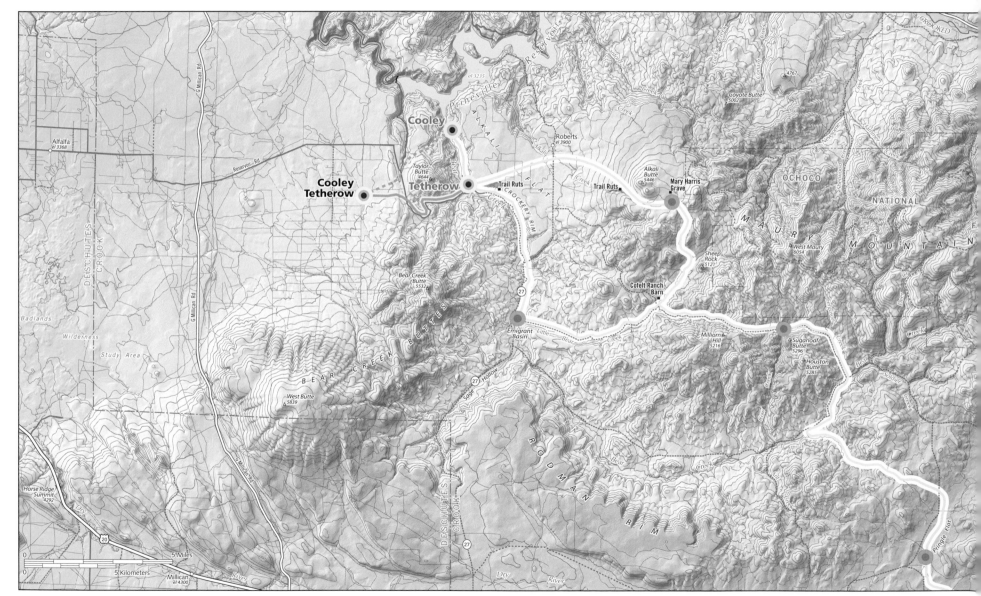

MAP 41 September 22, 1845

Aerial photo down Bear Creek from the Dunham Ranch to the Prineville Reservoir.

The Dunham Ranch. The paved road suggests a probable trail out of Bear Creek around the south end of Taylor Butte.

Cooley left Bear Creek and traveled ten miles.

IN HIS DIARY, COOLEY WRITES THAT HE TURNED to the right, but we believe his sense of direction failed him again. A right turn (going east) would have led up the very steep east side of Bear Creek, several miles north of the same steep area Tetherow had just descended the day before. In fact, Cooley's exit from his September 21 campsite is pure conjecture. An old county road runs from just south of the Prineville reservoir up and over the mesa rim. The road required considerable blasting and grading to be accessible in its prime. Without this roadwork, this canyon would have been impassable for wagons.

Slightly to the south is another canyon, which seemed also to be virtually impassable for wagons.

Cooley characterizes his trek out of the reservoir area as a "verry steep hill." It is difficult to imagine that he could have exited by way of this slope and there appears to be no other navigable exit from the west side of the Prineville Reservoir. We will probably never know his exact route on this day.

Local history suggests that at least one of the two companies, Cooley and Tetherow, exited Bear Creek around Taylor Butte. Certainly, this terrain would have made for an easier trail.

On September 25, Cooley refers to "the company behind." We suspect that Tetherow and Cooley remained close as they traversed the flat sagebrush-covered terrain toward the present-day small town of Alfalfa and beyond.

COOLEY: *Bad road to day. Weather fine. Come down the creek about 2 miles and then turned to the rite and left*

it after crossing it 3 times. Here wee had a verry steep hill to pull up and about 8 miles further struck a creek and camped in the forks. The creek wee camped on is to our rite. Some seder on the hills. The corse to whare wee left the creek is about west then about North to here.   10 miles

TUESDAY, SEPTEMBER 23

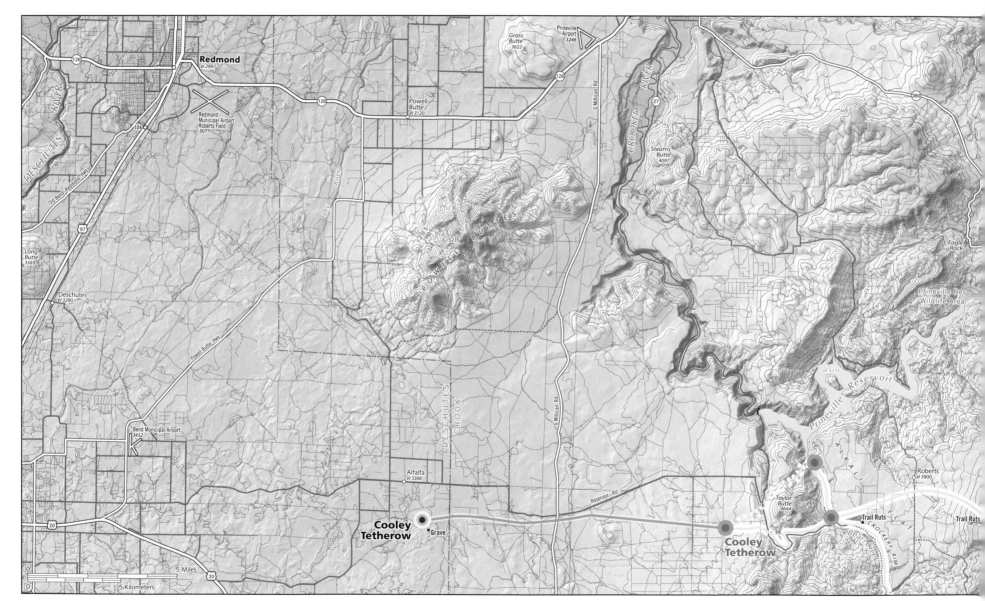

MAP 42 September 23, 1845

Grave near Alfalfa.

A close-up of the grave headstone.

An aerial view of the gravesite.

Cooley traveled twelve miles in a westerly direction.

- -

EXPEDITION MEMBERS BELIEVE COOLEY CAMPED near the present-day town of Alfalfa. Two or three miles southwest of Alfalfa a marked grave is located along an irrigation ditch. The memorial on the grave reads "Sacred to the Memory of JE IE with the Lost Meek Wagon Train of 1845." It is a beautiful site with an open meadow and juniper trees surrounding the grave.

Attached to the gravestone is a box with a little piece of paper which says the decedent was nineteen years old. Although we found no further information at the site, W. E. Searcy of Bend had written the following comment in an April 25, 1926, letter to the *Oregonian*: "W. H. Staats first saw this grave 46 years ago [1880]. He remembers the date on the tree, burned on with a hot iron and now faded by the elements as being 1845 or 1846. . . . Part of the inscription on the tree can still be read. It is 'Sacred to the Memory of JE—IE.' There is more but it cannot be made out."

COOLEY: *The road to day has been tolerable good. Weather fine. Crossed the creek this morning near its mouth whare it runs into the same creek wee have been traveling down and come about 3 miles down the creek here leaving it to our left and have traveled about a South West corse. About 3 miles from whare wee left the creek is a spring and plenty of grass and some few willow. Camped about 8 miles further at a branch or spring. Plenty of grass and some seder wood on the hills to the left about ¼ mile.   12 miles*

WEDNESDAY, SEPTEMBER 24

Cooley traveled twelve miles in a general northwesterly direction.

- -

COOLEY HAD HOPED TO STRIKE THE DESCHUTES River, but did not reach the river that evening and suffered through a dry camp.

While camped on the evening of the twenty-fourth, an emigrant, or emigrants, apparently carved "1845 Lost Meeks" on a juniper limb. Today that limb is on display in the Deschutes County Historical Society in Bend. Although the tree has long disappeared, an iron post just southeast of the Pronghorn real estate development marks the site and is inscribed as follows: "Message carved on limb of this tree by members of 1845 Oregon Immigrant Wagon Train. Piloted by Stephen Meek."

While some historians doubt the limb's authenticity, its location is directly on the line of travel from the site of the Alfalfa grave to Cline Falls near Redmond, Oregon. Moreover, its location corresponds to Cooley's mileage and campsite data. Since

"1845 Lost Meeks" limb.

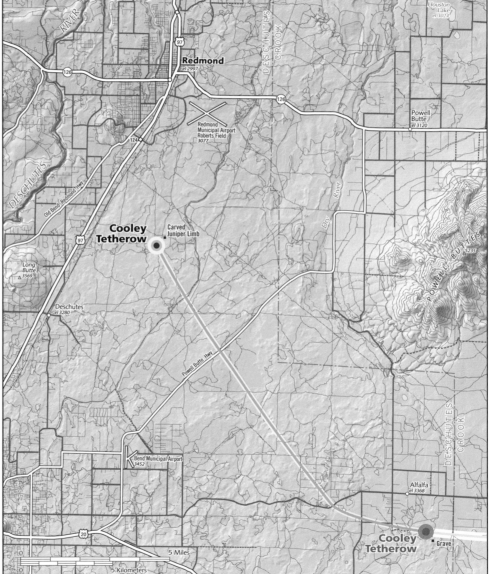

MAP 43 September 24, 1845

146

Pronghorn real estate development several miles southeast of Redmond. The site of the tree limb is just out of the frame in the lower right-hand corner.

Some members of the expedition at the limb site.

Cooley's diary was not known until after the limb was found in 1949, it seems highly unlikely that a fraudulent carver could have located it so precisely in the line of travel. An article from the *Bend Bulletin* of April 27, 1949, announces the discovery of the limb:

> Cut into the partly dead limb of a massive, aged juniper some ten miles east of Bend are a date and a name that have intrigued students of the early-day history of Central Oregon. The date is 1845 and the name, as nearly as can be deciphered, is "Josta Meeks." The limb, part of a tree that is 1 ½ feet 7 inches in circumference at the base, is six feet above the ground. Near the base of the tree are some stones which, it is believed, might have been used in preparing a campfire. . . The huge juniper was independently found in recent weeks by two Bend residents, Fred Carter and R. R. Edwards.

COOLEY: *The road to day has been tolerable good. Weather fine. Traveled about a North west corse for about 10 mile then turned about West with the expectation of striking the river but did not strike and stopped without any water.   12 miles*

THURSDAY, SEPTEMBER 25

Cooley traveled eight miles and camped about a mile and a half from the Deschutes River.

COOLEY'S COMPANY DROVE THEIR CATTLE TO THE river. A cursory look at the Deschutes River Valley from Bend to Redmond indicates that Cline Falls is the only break in the rim where animals could have come to drink.

Some two hundred yards northeast of the old Brand Restaurant on the Bend-Redmond highway about three or four miles south of Redmond, the expedition discovered a pile of rocks that looks very much like a grave. The pile, several feet long, could cover a human body. Years ago, Del Hinshaw located this gravesite and associated it with Meek. From Cooley's mileage records, we infer that his party camped several miles northwest of the graves near the Deschutes River, as he notes that his company had to drive cattle to the river.

In his confusing diary entry Cooley writes, "The rite hand road is some nearest as the company behind made a cut off on us." This suggests that Tetherow's company continued to be associated with Cooley's group as they reached the Deschutes and headed north.

While some historians, including Keith Clark and Lowell Tiller, believe that the wagons reached the Deschutes River at Bend, expedition members Bob Boyd, Steve Lent, and I are convinced that the

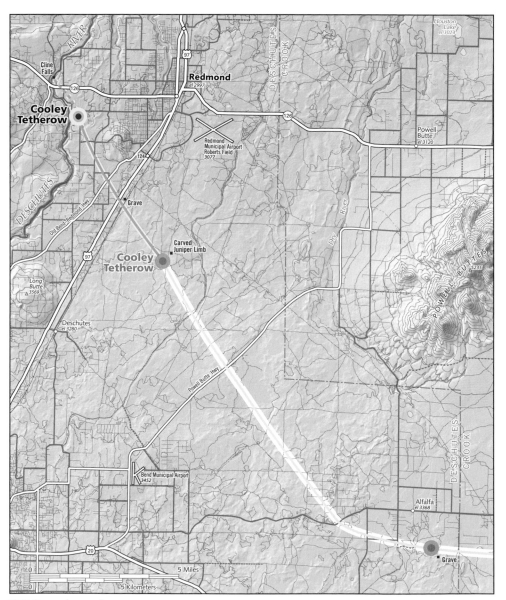

MAP 44 September 25, 1845

Cline Falls.

An aerial view of Cline Falls clearly showing the break in the east side of the rimrock in the vicinity of the bridge. The break would have permitted cattle and animals to get to the Deschutes River.

Unmarked grave.

emigrants traveled to Cline Falls. Steve Lent notes that it "does not seem logical that they would have landed at such a paradise and not ever mentioned it—particularly Cooley."

At this point, the Meek Research Expedition concluded its work. The survivors of both the northern and southern route Meek Cutoff parties had reached water and were no longer lost. One group was heading down the Crooked River and, of course, Cooley was on the Deschutes. Both still had many arduous days of travel ahead of them to get to The Dalles, but the most difficult part of the trail was behind them.

COOLEY: *The road to day has been tolerable good except some few rockey places. Weather fine. This morning wee started early and traveled nearly North for about 8 mile and camped on the hill about 1-1/2 mile from Shoots or Fales River and drove our cattle down a hollow to water. Some seder wood here and some grass. The rite hand road is some nearest as the company behind made a cut off on us. 8 miles*

SOME FINAL THOUGHTS

WEAKENED BY THEIR EXPERIENCES, THE EMI-grants struggled into western Oregon. Samuel Parker and his remaining family canoed down the Columbia River from The Dalles. The concluding entry in his diary is a poignant testament to the kinds of sufferings the emigrants endured:

thare [The Dalles] my wife and Child died and I staid till the 3 of November when I left fore oregon City in A large Canoe with four indiens for which I give sixty dollars   when I Started the wet wether had set in   I did not expect to git to the City with my fore sick Children and my oldes girl that was sick   I was looking all the time fore hir to die   I tuck my seete in the Canoe by hir and held hir up and the same at nite   when I come to the Cascade Falls I had to make A portige of 3 miles   I put my sick girl in A blanket and pack hir and onely rested once that day we maid the portige with the help of my fore indiens and my oldest boy and oldest girl boath had never been sick one minet on the Road   On the 8 I landed at oregon City wet hungry and all most wore out with my family most all sick   the 3 youngest soon got well but it was 19 days after I landed till my oldest stood alone   harty and well now.

A spring on the Double O Ranch.

The emigrants, while genuine pioneers, were not people living or working on the frontier of important discoveries. For the most part, they were common folk, often farmers, who simply wanted a better life and were willing to risk everything for that opportunity.

Perhaps Walt Whitman's words are an appropriate end to this story:

Not for delectations sweet,
Not the cushion and the slipper, not the peaceful and the studious,
Not the riches safe and palling, not for us the tame enjoyment,
Pioneers! O pioneers!

NOTE ON SOURCES

IN PREPARATION FOR WRITING THIS BOOK, I CON-sulted a large number of historical sources. As I felt no need to "reinvent the wheel," the first section of this work draws heavily on *Terrible Trail: The Meek Cutoff, 1845* by Keith Clark and Lowell Tiller (Caldwell, ID: Caxton, 1966) and on *The Brazen Overlanders of 1845* by Donna Wojcik (Portland, 1976). These books thoroughly document the story of the wagon train and also provide comprehensive bibliographies that were most helpful. The highly readable *The Plains Across: The Overland Emigrants and the Trans-Mississippi West, 1840–60* by John Unruh Jr. (Urbana: University of Illinois Press, 1979) offers a wealth of valuable information on all aspects of the emigration on the Oregon Trail.

The original diaries that form the basis for the Day to Day section of the book were not available to me but I did have access to transcriptions. The legible section of John Herren's diary was published in the *Albany Daily Democrat* of January 1 and 2, 1891. Jesse Harritt's diary was published in the Transactions of the Thirty-Eighth and Thirty-Ninth Annual Reunions of the Oregon Pioneer Association (Portland, June 22, 1910, and June 21, 1911). James Field Jr.'s diary was published in the *Willamette Farmer*, Portland, beginning on April 18, 1879. A copy of Samuel Parker's diary is on file at the Oregon Historical Society library. The Cooley diary has not been published, but a transcribed copy was made available to me by expedition member Margi Heater, a descendant of Eli Cooley's brother.

In addition to the diaries, two significant reminiscences written long after the events added considerable description and color to our efforts: *Reminiscences of a Pioneer: Incidents in the Life of a Pioneer in Oregon and Idaho*, by W. A. Goulder (Boise, ID: T. Regan, 1909) and *The Narrative of Samuel Hancock of His Overland Journey to Oregon in 1845 and of His Pioneering in the Oregon Country, 1845 to 1860* (New York: R. M. McBride, 1927).

Steve Lent, expedition member and assistant director and historian of the A. R. Bowman Memorial Museum in Prineville, Oregon, has published several guides to selected sections of the western part of the Meek Cutoff. Armed with these publications and a detailed map, any interested person could locate bits of the trail. See especially *Following the Lost Meek Trail in Central Oregon* (Prinville, OR: Crook County Historical Society, 2000).

Fred Lockley's several books and *Oregon Historical Quarterly* articles include many informative interviews with pioneer families and their descendants. See especially the ones cited in the alphabetical listing below. Lockley's foresight—he saw several generations disappearing and spent part of his life recording their pioneer memories—will be of interest to professional and lay historians many years into the future.

This list of valuable sources would not be complete without including Stephen Hall Meek's *The Autobiography of a Mountain Man* (Pasadena, CA: Glen Dawson, 1948). Meek lived and worked in the American West for most of his life. His story probably reflects the life style of all those we call "mountain men."

In addition to these central works, and in addition to all the correspondence and newspaper articles cited in the text, I have quoted and/or utilized the sources listed below. With the exception of a few additional and/or subsequently discovered items, most of entries are drawn from the bibliographies accompanying Clark and Tiller's *Terrible Trail* and Wojcik's *The Brazen Overlanders of 1845*. These bibliographies, when taken together, are remarkable for their virtually all-encompassing listing of diaries, journals, books, periodicals, manuscripts, and newspaper articles relating to the story of the Meek Cutoff.

BOOKS, ARTICLES, AND PAMPHLETS

Bancroft, Hubert Howe. *History of Oregon*, vol. 1. San Francisco: History Company, 1886.

Barlow, William A. "Reminiscences of Seventy Years." *Oregon Historical Quarterly* 13 (September 1912).

Gaston, Joseph. *The Centennial History of Oregon, 1811–1911.* Chicago, 1912.

Greenhow, Robert. *The History of Oregon and California, and the Other Territories on the north-west Coast of North America.* Boston, 1845. See especially the large map entitled "Map of the Western and Middle Portion of North America."

History of the Pacific Northwest: Oregon and Washington, vol 2. Portland, OR: North Pacific History Company, 1889.

An Illustrated History of Baker, Grant, Malheur and Harney Counties. Spokane, WA: Western Historical Publishing Co., 1902.

An Illustrated History of Central Oregon. Spokane: Western Historical Publishing Co., 1905.

Lent, Steve, *Following the Lost Meek Trail in Central Oregon* Prineville, OR: Crook County Historical Society, 2000.

Lockley, Fred. "The McNemees and Tetherows with the Migration of 1845." *Oregon Historical Quarterly* 25, no. 4 (December 1924).

———. *Visionaries, Mountain Men & Empire Builders,* vol. 3. Eugene: Oregon County Library, 1982.

———. *Voices of the Oregon Territory, Conversations with Bullwhackers, Muleskinners, Pioneers, Prospectors, '49ers, Indian Fighters, Trappers, Ex Barkeepers, Authors, Preachers, Poets and New Poets & All Sorts & Conditions of Men.* Compiled and edited by Mike Helm. Eugene, OR: Rainy Day Press, 1981.

McNary, Lawrence A. "Route of the Meek Cut-Off, 1845." *Oregon Historical Quarterly* 35, no. 1 (March 1934).

McNeal, William H. *History of Wasco County, Oregon.* The Dalles, OR: B. Harris, 1952.

Menefee, Leah Collins, and Lowell Tiller. "Cutoff Fever." *Oregon Historical Quarterly* (beginning in vol. 76, December 1976, and continuing through vol. 79, no. 1 [Spring 1978]).

Munson, Myron A. *The Munson Record: A Genealogical and Biographical Account of Captain Thomas Munson and His Descendants,* vol. 1. New Haven, CT, 1895.

Palmer, Joel. "Journal of Travels over the Rocky Mountains, 1845–1846." In Reuben Gold Thwaites, *Early Western Travels, 1748–1846,* vol. 30. Cleveland, OH: A. H. Clark, 1906. Includes Palmer's "Necessary Outfits for Emigrants Traveling to Oregon."

Polk County Pioneer Sketches, vol. 1. Dallas, OR, 1927.

MISCELLANEOUS

Cochran, J. Nelson. "History of Blue Bucket Gold Hunt Which Took Place in May and June 1860 by a Company of 52 Men." Manuscript 1045 in the Oregon Historical Society Library, Portland.

Hembree, W. H. (Captain). "Pioneer and Gold Mining Lore." Interview by A. C. Sherbert of the Federal Writers' Project, Works Progress Administration, April 28, 1938. Oregon Folklore Studies.

Hinshaw, Del. "Tetherow West." Six-page typescript from a file maintained by Del Hinshaw and a copy in the author's possession.

King, Stephen, and Mariah King. "King Burial and a Letter." Typed copy made verbatim on July 27, 1925, of a letter written in 1846. From the files of the Oregon Historical Society. Document Code 45KIN02.

McClure, Andrew S. "The Diary of Andrew S. McClure," Reproduced by the Lane County Pioneer Historical Society, Eugene, OR, 1959.

"Probably from Tetherow Journal—Members of Cumberland Presbyterian Church." A typewritten document furnished to the author by Donna Wojcik.

Walter, W. W. "Reminiscences of an Old 45er." From the files of the Oregon Historical Society Research Library. Document Code 45WAL01.

INDEX

A

Albany Daily Democrat, 93, 152
Alec Butte, 93, 97
Alfalfa, 143, 145–46
alkali, 85, 90, 93, 97, 140
Alkali Butte, 12, 25, 134–38, 140
Alkali Creek, 138, 140
Alkali Flat, 93, 140
Allan Cartography, 16
American Fur Company, 33

B

balm, 44, 60–61
Barlow, William, 8, 10
Bayley, Elizabeth, 106, 119
Bear Creek, 130, 134–35, 140, 143
Bend, 12, 16, 21–22, 114, 122, 145–48
Bendire Ridge, 53–54, 58–59
Beulah, 20, 57–58, 60–61, 65
Blue Bucket, ix, 14, 23–24, 28, 70, 134–37
Blue Mountains, 8, 10, 34, 44, 51, 61, 64, 68, 75–76
boiling springs, 43–44
Boise River, 34, 54, 61, 88, 94
Boise Valley, 8
Boyd, Bob, 16, 21–22, 36, 44, 48, 58, 66, 148
Brazen Overlanders of 1845, The, 10, 87, 152
Brigham Young University, 20
Buckaroo Springs, 53
Buck Creek, 111, 116–17, 120
Bully Creek, 39–41
Bully Creek Reservoir Park, 39–40
Bureau of Land Management (BLM), 16, 19, 21, 33, 44, 58
Burns, 21, 78, 81, 85, 122
Burnt River, 8, 34, 51
Butler Beulah Ranch, 57
Butterfly Springs, 53

C

Calf Creek, 132, 134
California, 3, 13–15, 18, 22, 24, 48, 70, 76
Cascade Range or mountains, 10, 17, 25, 76, 79–84, 88, 103, 107, 138
Castle Rock, 53–54, 61–66, 74–75
Cayuse Indians, 8, 10, 75
Cemetery Ridge, 125, 130
chalk bluffs, 43
Chambers, Sarah, 75–76
Clark, Keith, ix, 7–8, 13, 15, 23, 25, 57, 93, 122, 148, 152
clevis, 44
Cline Falls, x, 12–13, 30, 146, 148–150
Clover Creek, 120, 122–123, 126
Coffelt Ranch, 134–136
Columbia River, ix, 8, 10, 12, 34, 37, 75–76, 79–80, 84, 151
Conestoga, 6
Cooley, Christopher, 21
Cooley, Eli, 14–16, 21, 30–31, 34, 36–37, 39–40, 43–44, 47–48, 53–55, 57–65, 68–69, 71, 73, 76, 78–82, 84–85, 88, 90–91, 93–94, 97–98, 101–5, 107–110, 112–117, 119–120, 122–23, 125–27, 130, 132, 134–35, 138, 140–41, 143, 145–48, 150, 152
Cottonwood Creek, 25, 65–68
Cow Creek, 25, 78–79, 130, 132, 134, 138
Crockery Rim, 140–41
Cronin, Paul, 21, 23, 32, 47, 66
Crooked River, x, 12–13, 25, 79, 81, 83, 88, 103, 107, 120, 122, 125, 130, 136, 150
Cumberland Presbyterian Church, 3

D

Dalles, The, ix, 8, 10, 12–14, 16, 23, 25, 34, 37, 75–76, 130, 136, 150–51
Danger Point, 43–44, 47
Dayton, Oregon, 7

D (continued)

Deschutes River, ix–x, 8, 10, 12, 16, 25, 30, 75–76, 79, 88, 103, 132, 136, 146, 148, 150
Dog Mountain, 85, 87
Donner Party, 3
Double O Ranch, 90–91, 93, 97
drean, 30, 44, 71, 76, 80, 84, 91
Dunham Ranch, 135, 140–41, 143

E

Egli Reservoir, 98–99
Egli Ridge, 98
Egli Spring, 97–99, 101–2
Elliott, Elijah, 17, 88
Emigrant Basin, 134, 140
Emigrant Hill, 57

F

Ferguson Creek, 130, 132
Field, James, Jr., 14–15, 31–32, 34, 36–37, 39–40, 43–44, 47–48, 53–55, 57–65, 68–69, 71, 73, 76, 78–85, 87–88, 90–91, 93, 95, 97, 99, 101–5, 107–17, 119–20, 122–23, 125, 127, 130, 132, 152
Fort Boise, 7–10, 15, 31–34, 37, 76, 104
Fort Hall, 8, 13, 33, 62, 101
Fort Harney, 78
Fort Laramie, 10, 76
Fort Vancouver, 8, 10
Fort Walla Walla, 37
Fremont, John C., 61
Fremont's Peak, 53, 61, 64, 68, 73, 80

G

Gesner, Alonzo, 130–131
GI Ranch, 12, 16, 21, 111, 113–14, 116–17, 120–23, 125, 130
Glass Butte, 12, 110–11, 114, 117–19
gold, ix, 14–15, 21, 23–25, 28, 33, 70, 93, 126, 134, 136–38

Goulder, W. A., 8, 12, 15, 47, 73, 83, 111, 152
Grand Ronde Valley, 8, 10
Great Salt Lake, 20
Greenhow, Robert, 18
Gregory Creek, 54

H

Hall, Lawrence (Captain), 115
Hall, Lucy Jane, 115
Hampton Butte, 12, 25–26, 28, 117, 122
Hancock, Samuel, 7, 15, 32, 47–48, 58, 66–67, 102–104, 112, 114–15, 117, 152
Harney Lake, 12, 17, 85–88, 90, 93–94
Harney Valley, 12, 17, 25, 79–83, 88
Harper, 39, 43–44, 48
Harris, Mary E., 136–137
Harritt, Jesse, 14–15, 31, 34, 36, 39–40, 43–44, 47, 51, 53–55, 57–65, 68–69, 71, 73, 76, 78–85, 88, 90–91, 93, 95, 97, 99, 101–13, 115–17, 119–20, 122–23, 125, 127, 130, 132, 152
Hay Creek Valley, 12
Heater, Margi, 21, 44, 70, 152
Hembree, W. H. (Captain), 23
Herren, Daniel, 24, 135, 137
Herren, John Daniel (also Herron), 14–16, 24, 30–31, 34, 36–37, 39–40, 43–44, 47–48, 50, 53–54, 57–58, 60–61, 63–71, 73, 75–76, 78–83, 85, 88, 90–91, 93–94, 97, 102, 120, 122, 135, 137, 152
Herren, W. H., 24, 28, 135–36, 141
Herren, W. J., 24, 135
High Desert Museum, 16, 21–22
Hinshaw, Del, 16, 22–23, 39, 43, 48, 53–54, 58, 64, 66, 73, 75, 93, 97, 105–6, 117, 122–23, 134, 136, 138, 148
Houston Butte, 132
Hudson's Bay Company, ix, 8, 34

I

Indians, ix, 3, 8, 10, 12, 25, 34, 36–37, 67, 70, 75, 80, 84, 95, 99, 107, 136, 151
Iron Mountain, 90–91, 93, 97

J

Jay's River, 75–76, 79–81, 83, 91, 103
Jefferson, Thomas, 20
John Day River, 76, 79, 81, 83–84, 88, 103
Jordan, Bob and Brad, 40

K

Keeney, Jonathan, 33
Keeney Pass, 32–34
king bolt, 105, 107
Klondike Kate, 126

L

Lent, Steve, 14, 16, 21–22, 33, 48, 57, 66, 70, 97, 122, 125, 130, 135, 148, 150, 152
Lockley, Fred, 25, 79, 152
Lost Creek, 102–106, 108–111, 113–117
Lost Wagon Train, ix, 7, 14, 23, 75, 108

M

Macy, William, 17
Madras, x, 12, 120, 123
Malheur Lake, 12, 17, 81, 86–88
Malheur National Wildlife Refuge, 85, 90
Malheur River, 8, 10, 12, 24–25, 27, 31, 34, 36–37, 39–40, 43–44, 58, 60–65, 67–69, 71, 75–76, 80, 84, 103, 132, 137
Maury Mountains, x, 12, 25–26, 30, 120, 130
McClure, Andrew S., 17
McCormack Ranch, 130, 132
McEldowney, Art and Jane, 16, 21, 44, 48
McNamee, Job, 106

McNary, James, 14–15
Meacham, Jim, 16
Meek, Stephen S., ix–x, 3, 7–8, 10, 12–15, 17–18, 20–23, 32–34, 36–37, 39–40, 47, 66–67, 70, 75–76, 78–79, 86–88, 102–3, 105–6, 108–15, 117, 119, 127, 146–48, 152
Meek Cutoff, ix–x, 6, 12–17, 22–23, 32, 70, 76, 87–88, 104, 135, 150, 152
Meek's Gulch, 65–66
Meek Trail, ix, 10, 17, 21–23, 57, 70, 79, 122, 125, 130, 152
Menefee, Leah Collins, 23, 87–88
Metolius, 25, 136
Midnight Point, 111, 117
Miller, Ron, 140
Milliorn Hill, 134–35
Misery Flat, 118
Missouri, ix, 3–4, 7–8, 14, 137
Morris Bishop, Ellen, 22
Mount Hood, 13

N

Northern Pacific Railroad, 3
Nye Ranch, 135

O

Oard Flat, 78–80
odometer, 20, 47, 58, 60, 65, 78–79, 81, 93, 101, 122, 125
Olney, Nathan, 8, 10
Ontario, Oregon, 15, 31
Oregon California Trails Association, 48, 76
Oregon City, 9, 13–15, 151
Oregon Emigrating Company, 6–7
Oregon Historical Society, 22, 152
Oregonian, The, 24, 76, 112, 122, 135–37, 145
Oregon Pioneer Association, 152
Oregon Society Constitution, 6
Oregon Spectator, 7

Oregon Territory, ix, 3, 7, 14–15, 18

Oregon Trail, 3–4, 8–9, 14, 31–34, 36, 76, 152

O'Toole Ranch, 69–71, 73–75

Ownbey (also Owensby), Nicholas, 15, 37, 47, 88, 97, 101–5, 107–8, 110, 112–13, 115

oxen, 6, 12, 24, 34, 36, 48, 54–55, 61–62, 64, 76, 83, 88, 94, 101, 106, 108–109, 115, 118–19, 136

P

Pacific Northwest, ix, 8, 18

Packwood, 93, 99

Paiute Indians, 12, 70

Palmer, Joel, 7, 13, 31–32

Parker, Samuel, 7, 12, 14–16, 31, 34, 36–37, 39–40, 43–44, 47–48, 53–55, 57–65, 68–69, 71, 73, 76, 78–81, 83–85, 88, 90–91, 93–94, 97–98, 101–4, 107–10, 112–13, 115–18, 120, 122–23, 125, 127, 130, 132, 151–52

Payette River, 8

Pilot Butte, 25, 136

Pine Creek, 25, 73, 78

pit house, 70–71

Plains Across, The, 3, 152

Pole Creek, 53

Portland, 3, 8, 22, 127, 152

Portland Daily Bee, 24

prairie schooner, 6

Prineville, 14, 21, 25, 122, 136, 140–141, 143, 152

Pringle Flat, 125–128

R

Ragen, Brooks, 22

Ragen, Suzanne, 22, 66

Redmond, x, 12, 146–148

Riggs, James B., 15, 37, 107, 109, 114, 117, 119

Rock Creek, 78

Rubbert ranch, 135

ruts, x, 16–17, 33–34, 36, 39, 43–45, 48–50, 53–54, 57, 61, 63, 66–68, 70–71, 74, 78–79, 83, 97–98, 117, 122, 126, 130, 134–35, 140

S

sage, 12, 37, 61, 73, 82–83, 88, 90–91, 94, 115, 117, 119, 123

sagebrush, 10, 19, 30, 33, 36, 39, 43–44, 48, 57, 70, 73–74, 83, 90–91, 93, 97, 117, 122, 125, 134, 136, 143

Sagebrush Springs, x, 12, 120

Sand Hollow, 120, 122–23, 125–26

Schaefer, Lee and Lynn, 22

Shaniko Flat, 12

Sheep Rock, 134–36

Sherars Bridge, 12

Silver Creek, 93

Silver Lake, 12, 90, 93–94, 97

Silvies River, 12, 81–83, 87–88

Sinks of Lost Creek, 104, 105, 108, 113–14, 116

Smith, Jack, 78

Snake River, 7–8, 10, 15, 31–32, 34, 36, 40, 103

Spring Creek, 43

springs, x, 12, 15, 25, 33–34, 39–40, 43–44, 48, 53–55, 57–60, 62, 73, 79–80, 90–91, 93–94, 97–99, 101–4, 107–9, 111, 113–17, 120–23, 125, 127, 130, 145

Steens Mountain, 25, 79–82

Steens Ridge, 125–28

Stinking Hollow, 106, 114

Stinkingwater Mountains, 10, 25, 79

Sugarloaf Butte, 132

Swamp Creek, 47, 53, 57

T

Taylor Butte, 143

Terrible Trail: The Meek Cutoff, 15, 122, 152

Tetherow, Solomon (also Teatherow and Tethrow), 3, 7, 15, 24, 28, 75, 109–10, 112–17, 120, 122–23, 125, 130, 132, 134–38, 140, 143, 148

Tiller, Lowell, ix–x, 7–8, 13, 15, 23, 25, 57, 87–88, 93, 122, 148, 152

Trout Creek, 12

Turner Ranch, 65–66, 68–69

T'Vault, W. G., 7

Tygh Valley, 25, 136

U

University of Oregon, 16

Unruh, John D., Jr., 3, 6, 152

U.S. Army, 16, 20, 57

V

Vale, ix–x, 8, 12–13, 15, 17, 23, 31, 33–34, 36–37, 39, 75–76, 88, 130

Vines Hill, 39

W

Wagontire Mountain, 12, 28, 91, 94, 97–98, 102–5, 110, 114

Walla Walla Indians, 8, 10, 37

Warm Spring Indians, 25, 136

Warm Springs Creek, 57–58

Westfall, 20, 40, 43–44, 47–48

Westfall Butte, 48, 51, 53–55, 58, 61, 67

Whitman, Marcus, 22

Whitman, Walt, 151

Willamette River, ix, 13, 76

Willamette Valley, ix, 7, 13–14, 17, 23, 75, 103

Wojcik, Donna, ix–x, 3, 10, 87, 152

Wright, Dr. Norman E., 20

Wright's Point, 81–85, 88